Moreton Morrell Site

STRATEGIC HUMAN RESOURCE MANAGEMENT

WARWICKSHIRE COLLEGE LIBRARY

For free online support material please go to the Kogan Page website:
www.koganpage.com / strategichrm
Password: SHRM53756

STRATEGIC HUMAN RESOURCE MANAGEMENT

A GUIDE TO ACTION

4TH EDITION

Michael Armstrong

**KOGAN
PAGE**

London and Philadelphia

First published in Great Britain and the United States in 1992 as *Human Resource Management: Strategy and Action*
Second edition published as *Strategic Human Resource Management: A Guide to Action* 2000
Third edition 2006
Reprinted 2006
Fourth edition 2008

Kogan Page Limited
120 Pentonville Road
London N1 9JN
United Kingdom
www.koganpage.com

Kogan Page US
525 South 4th Street, #241
Philadelphia PA 19147
USA

© Michael Armstrong, 1992, 2000, 2006, 2008

ISBN 978 0 7494 5375 6

British Library Cataloguing-in-Publication Data

A CIP record for this book is available from the British Library.

Library of Congress Cataloging-in-Publication Data

Armstrong, Michael, 1928–
    Strategic human resource management : a guide to action / Michael Armstrong. -- 4th ed.
        p. cm
    Includes bibliographical references and index.
    ISBN 978-0-7494-5375-6
  1. Personnel management.   I. Title
    HF5549.A89784 2008
    658.3'01--dc22

                                                                                    2008017601

Typeset by Saxon Graphics Ltd, Derby
Printed and bound in India by Replika Press Pvt Ltd

Contents

PART 2 THE PRACTICE OF STRATEGIC HRM

PART 3 HR STRATEGIES

PART 4 THE STRATEGIC HR TOOLKIT

Introduction

Strategic human resource management (SHRM) is an approach to the development and implementation of HR strategies that are integrated with business strategies and enable the organization to achieve its goals.

In essence, strategic HRM is conceptual; it is a general notion of how integration or 'fit' between HR and business strategies is achieved, the benefits of taking a longer-term view of where HR should be going and how to get there, and how coherent and mutually supporting HR strategies should be developed and implemented. Importantly, it is also about how members of the HR function should adopt a strategic approach on a day-to-day basis. This means that they operate as part of the management team, ensure that HR activities support the achievement of business strategies on a continuous basis and are consciously concerned with seeing that their activities add value.

To understand strategic HRM it is first necessary to appreciate the concepts of human resource management and strategy as covered in Chapters 1 and 2 respectively in Part 1 (the framework of strategic HR). The concept of strategic human resource management (strategic HRM) is then examined in detail in Chapter 3.

Part 2 of the book is concerned with the roles of management and HR in strategic HRM and with the processes of developing and implementing HR strategies. Part 3 covers each of the main areas of HR in which strategies are developed. The book concludes with a toolkit providing guidance on developing HR strategy through a strategic review.

Part 1

The conceptual framework of strategic HRM

1

The concept of human resource management

In the first section of this chapter human resource management (HRM) is defined in general and as a system. Its aims and characteristics are described in later sections of the chapter.

HRM DEFINED

Human resource management is defined as a strategic and coherent approach to the management of an organization's most valued assets – the people working there, who individually and collectively contribute to the achievement of its objectives.

Boxall *et al* (2007) describe HRM as 'the management of work and people towards desired ends'. John Storey (1989) believes that HRM can be regarded as a 'set of interrelated policies with an ideological and philosophical underpinning'. He suggests four aspects that constitute the *meaningful* version of HRM: 1) a particular constellation of beliefs and assumptions; 2) a strategic thrust informing decisions about people management; 3) the central involvement of line managers; and 4) reliance upon a set of 'levers' to shape the employment relationship. HRM is further defined by the two models of HRM developed by what might be described as its founding fathers.

The matching model of HRM

One of the first explicit statements of the HRM concept was made by the Michigan School (Fombrun, Tichy and Devanna, 1984). They held that HR systems and the organization structure should be managed in a way that is congruent with organizational strategy (hence the name 'matching model'). They further explained that there is a human resource cycle (an adaptation of which is illustrated in Figure 1.1), which consists of four generic processes or functions that are performed in all organizations. These are:

▮ *selection* – matching available human resources to jobs;
▮ *appraisal* – performance management;
▮ *rewards* – 'the reward system is one of the most under-utilized and mishandled managerial tools for driving organizational performance'; it must reward short- as well as long-term achievements, bearing in mind that 'business must perform in the present to succeed in the future';
▮ *development* – developing high-quality employees.

The Harvard framework

The other pioneers of HRM were the Harvard School of Beer *et al* (1984), who developed what Boxall (1992) calls the 'Harvard framework'. This framework is based on their belief that the problems of historical personnel management can only be solved:

when general managers develop a viewpoint of how they wish to see employees involved in and developed by the enterprise, and of what HRM

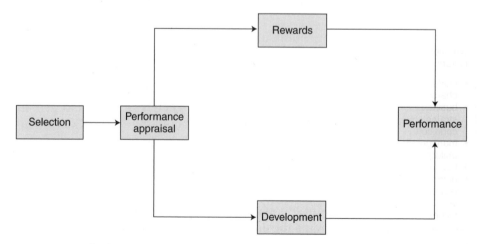

Figure 1.1 The human resource cycle
Source: Fombrun, Tichy and Devanna, 1984

policies and practices may achieve those goals. Without either a central philosophy or a strategic vision – which can be provided *only* by general managers – HRM is likely to remain a set of independent activities, each guided by its own practice tradition.

Beer and his colleagues believed that, 'Today, many pressures are demanding a broader, more comprehensive and more strategic perspective with regard to the organization's human resources.' These pressures have created a need for 'A longer-term perspective in managing people and consideration of people as potential assets rather than merely a variable cost'. They were the first to underline the HRM tenet that it belongs to line managers. They also stated that 'Human resource management involves all management decisions and action that affect the nature of the relationship between the organization and its employees – its human resources.'

The Harvard school suggested that HRM had two characteristic features: 1) line managers accept more responsibility for ensuring the alignment of competitive strategy and personnel policies; 2) personnel has the mission of setting policies that govern how personnel activities are developed and implemented in ways that make them more mutually reinforcing. The Harvard framework as modelled by Beer *et al* is shown in Figure 1.2.

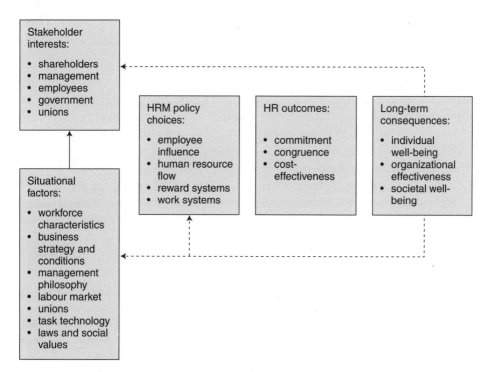

Figure 1.2 The Harvard framework for human resource management
Source: Beer *et al*, 1984

According to Boxall (1992) the advantages of this model are that it:

▌ incorporates recognition of a range of stakeholder interests;
▌ recognizes the importance of 'trade-offs', either explicitly or implicitly, between the interests of owners and those of employees as well as between various interest groups;
▌ widens the context of HRM to include 'employee influence', the organization of work and the associated question of supervisory style;
▌ acknowledges a broad range of contextual influences on management's choice of strategy, suggesting a meshing of both product-market and socio-cultural logics;
▌ emphasizes strategic choice – it is not driven by situational or environmental determinism.

HRM is seen in the UK 'as a substantially different model built on unitarism, individualism, high commitment and strategic alignment' (Guest, 1987). However, the Harvard model has exerted considerable influence over the theory and practice of HRM, particularly in its emphasis on the fact that HRM is the concern of management in general rather than the HR function in particular. As Boxall, Purcell and Wright (2007) point out, 'HRM is not just what HR departments do.'

HUMAN RESOURCE SYSTEMS

Human resource management operates through human resource systems as illustrated in Figure 1.3. These bring together in a coherent way:

▌ *HR philosophies*, describing the overarching values and guiding principles adopted in managing people;
▌ *HR strategies*, defining the direction in which HRM intends to go;
▌ *HR policies*, which are the guidelines defining how these values, principles and strategies should be applied and implemented in specific areas of HRM;
▌ *HR processes*, consisting of the formal procedures and methods used to put HR strategic plans and policies into effect;
▌ *HR practices*, consisting of the informal approaches used in managing people;
▌ *HR programmes*, which enable HR strategies, policies and practices to be implemented according to plan.

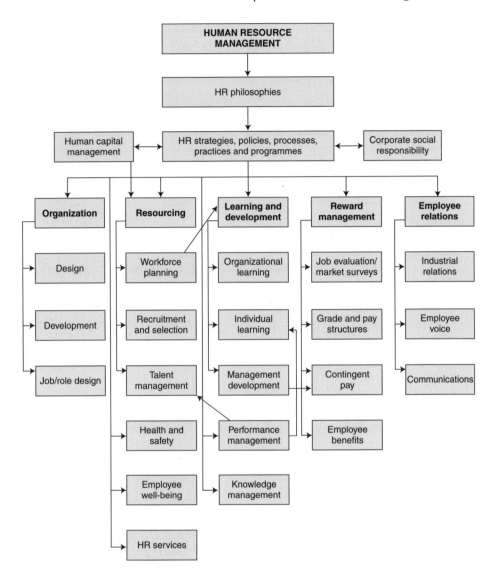

Figure 1.3 HRM activities

AIMS OF HRM

The overall purpose of human resource management is to ensure that the organization is able to achieve success through people. As Ulrich and Lake (1990) remark: 'HRM systems can be the source of organizational capabilities that allow firms to learn and capitalize on new opportunities.'

Dyer and Holder (1988) analyse management's HR goals under the dimensions of contribution (what kind of employee behaviour is expected?), composition (what headcount, staffing ratio and skill mix?), competence (what general level of ability is desired?) and commitment (what level of employee attachment and identification?).

Twelve policy goals for HRM have been identified by Caldwell (2004):

1. managing people as assets that are fundamental to the competitive advantage of the organization;
2. aligning HRM policies with business policies and corporate strategy;
3. developing a close fit of HR policies, procedures and systems with one another;
4. creating a flatter and more flexible organization capable of responding more quickly to change;
5. encouraging teamworking and cooperation across internal organizational boundaries;
6. creating a strong customer-first philosophy throughout the organization;
7. empowering employees to manage their own self-development and learning;
8. developing reward strategies designed to support a performance-driven culture;
9. improving employee involvement through better internal communication;
10. building greater employee commitment to the organization;
11. increasing line management responsibility for HR policies;
12. developing the facilitating role of managers as enablers.

But as Dyer and Holder (1988) emphasize: 'HRM goals vary according to competitive choices, technologies or service tangibles, characteristics of their employees (eg could be different for managers), the state of the labour market and the societal regulations and national culture.' And Boxall, Purcell and Wright (2007) note that 'The general motives of HRM are multiple.'

Specifically, HRM is concerned with achieving objectives in the areas summarized below.

Organizational effectiveness

'Distinctive human resource practices shape the core competencies that determine how firms compete' (Cappelli and Crocker-Hefter, 1996). Extensive research has shown that such practices can make a significant impact on firm performance. HRM strategies aim to support programmes for improving organizational effectiveness by developing policies in such areas as knowledge management, talent management and generally creating 'a great place to work'. This is the 'big idea' as described by Purcell *et al*

(2003), which consists of a 'clear vision and a set of integrated values'. More specifically, HR strategies can be concerned with the development of continuous improvement and customer relations policies.

Human capital management

The human capital of an organization consists of the people who work there and on whom the success of the business depends. It has been defined by Bontis *et al* (1999) as follows: 'Human capital represents the human factor in the organization; the combined intelligence, skills and expertise that gives the organization its distinctive character. The human elements of the organization are those that are capable of learning, changing, innovating and providing the creative thrust which if properly motivated can ensure the long-term survival of the organization.'

Human capital can be regarded as the prime asset of an organization, and businesses need to invest in that asset to ensure their survival and growth. HRM aims to ensure that the organization obtains and retains the skilled, committed and well-motivated workforce it needs. This means taking steps to assess and satisfy future people needs and to enhance and develop the inherent capacities of people – their contributions, potential and employability – by providing learning and continuous development opportunities. It involves the operation of 'rigorous recruitment and selection procedures, performance-contingent incentive compensation systems, and management development and training activities linked to the needs of the business' (Becker *et al*, 1997). It also means engaging in talent management – the process of acquiring and nurturing talent, wherever it is and wherever it is needed, by using a number of interdependent HRM policies and practices in the fields of resourcing, learning and development, performance management and succession planning.

The process of human capital management (HCM) as described in the next chapter is closely associated with human resource management. However, the focus of HCM is more on the use of metrics (measurements of HR and people performance) as a means of providing guidance on people management strategy and practice.

Knowledge management

Knowledge management is 'any process or practice of creating, acquiring, capturing, sharing and using knowledge, wherever it resides, to enhance learning and performance in organizations' (Scarborough *et al*, 1999). HRM aims to support the development of firm-specific knowledge and skills that are the result of organizational learning processes.

Reward management

HRM aims to enhance motivation, job engagement and commitment by introducing policies and processes that ensure that people are valued and rewarded for what they do and achieve and for the levels of skill and competence they reach.

Employee relations

The aim is to create a climate in which productive and harmonious relationships can be maintained through partnerships between management and employees and their trade unions.

Meeting diverse needs

HRM aims to develop and implement policies that balance and adapt to the needs of its stakeholders and provide for the management of a diverse workforce, taking into account individual and group differences in employment, personal needs, work style and aspirations and the provision of equal opportunities for all.

Bridging the gap between rhetoric and reality

The research conducted by Gratton *et al* (1999) found that there was generally a wide gap between the sort of rhetoric expressed above and reality. Managements may start with good intentions to do some or all of these things, but the realization of them – 'theory in use' – is often very difficult. This arises because of contextual and process problems: other business priorities, short-termism, limited support from line managers, an inadequate infrastructure of supporting processes, lack of resources, resistance to change and lack of trust. An overarching aim of HRM is to bridge this gap by making every attempt to ensure that aspirations are translated into sustained and effective action. To do this, members of the HR function have to remember that it is relatively easy to come up with new and innovatory policies and practice. The challenge is to get them to work. They must appreciate, in the phrase used by Purcell *et al* (2003), that it is the front-line managers who bring HR policies to life, and act accordingly.

CHARACTERISTICS OF HRM

The characteristics of the HRM concept are that it is:

▮ diverse;
▮ strategic, with an emphasis on integration;

▌ commitment-orientated;

▌ based on the belief that people should be treated as assets (human capital);

▌ unitarist rather than pluralist, individualistic rather than collective, in its approach to employee relations;

▌ a management-driven activity – the delivery of HRM is a line management responsibility;

▌ focused on business values, although this emphasis is being modified in some quarters and more recognition is being given to the importance of moral and social values.

The diversity of HRM

There are no universal characteristics of HRM. Many models exist, and practices within different organizations are diverse, often corresponding to the conceptual version of HRM in only a few respects. As Boxall *et al* (2007) remark: 'Human resource management covers a vast array of activities and shows a huge range of variations across occupations, organizational levels, business units, firms, industries and societies.'

Hendry and Pettigrew (1990) play down the prescriptive element of the HRM model and extend the analytical elements. As pointed out by Boxall (1992), such an approach rightly avoids labelling HRM as a single form and advances more slowly by proceeding more analytically. It is argued by Hendry and Pettigrew that 'better descriptions of structures and strategy-making in complex organizations, and of frameworks for understanding them, are an essential underpinning for HRM'.

A distinction was made by Storey (1989) between the 'hard' and 'soft' versions of HRM. The hard version of HRM emphasizes that people are important resources through which organizations achieve competitive advantage. These resources have therefore to be acquired, developed and deployed in ways that will benefit the organization. The focus is on the quantitative, calculative and business-strategic aspects of managing human resources in as 'rational' a way as for any other economic factor. As Guest (1999) comments, 'The drive to adopt HRM is… based on the business case of a need to respond to an external threat from increasing competition. It is a philosophy that appeals to managements who are striving to increase competitive advantage and appreciate that to do this they must invest in human resources as well as new technology.' He also comments that HRM 'reflects a long-standing capitalist tradition in which the worker is regarded as a commodity'. The emphasis is therefore on the interests of management, integration with business strategy, obtaining added value from people by the processes of human resource development and performance management, and the need for a strong corporate culture expressed in mission and value statements and reinforced by communications, training and performance management processes.

The soft version of HRM traces its roots to the human-relations school; it emphasizes communication, motivation and leadership. As described by Storey (1989), it involves 'treating employees as valued assets, a source of competitive advantage through their commitment, adaptability and high quality (of skills, performance and so on)'. It therefore views employees, in the words of Guest (1999), as means rather than objects, but it does not go as far as following Kant's (2003 [1781]) advice: 'Treat people as ends unto themselves rather than as means to an end.' The soft approach to HRM stresses the need to gain the commitment – the 'hearts and minds' – of employees through involvement, communications and other methods of developing a high-commitment, high-trust organization. Attention is also drawn to the key role of organizational culture.

In 1998, Karen Legge defined the 'hard' model of HRM as a process emphasizing 'the close integration of human resource policies with business strategy which regards employees as a resource to be managed in the same rational way as any other resource being exploited for maximum return'. In contrast, the soft version of HRM sees employees as 'valued assets and as a source of competitive advantage through their commitment, adaptability and high level of skills and performance'.

It has, however, been observed by Truss (1999) that, 'even if the rhetoric of HRM is soft, the reality is often hard, with the interests of the organization prevailing over those of the individual'. And research carried out by Gratton *et al* (1999) found that, in the eight organizations they studied, a mixture of hard and soft HRM approaches was identified. This suggested to the researchers that the distinction between hard and soft HRM was not as precise as some commentators have implied.

The strategic nature of HRM

Perhaps the most significant feature of HRM is the importance attached to strategic integration, which flows from top management's vision and leadership, and which requires the full commitment of people to it. David Guest (1987, 1989a, 1989b, 1991) believes that this is a key policy goal for HRM, which is concerned with the ability of the organization to integrate HRM issues into its strategic plans, to ensure that the various aspects of HRM cohere, and to encourage line managers to incorporate an HRM perspective into their decision making.

Karen Legge (1989) considers that one of the common themes of the typical definitions of HRM is that human resource policies should be integrated with strategic business planning. Keith Sisson (1990) suggests that a feature increasingly associated with HRM is a stress on the integration of HR policies both with one another and with business planning more generally.

John Storey (1989) suggests that 'The concept locates HRM policy formulation firmly at the strategic level and insists that a characteristic of HRM is its internally coherent approach.'

The commitment-orientated nature of HRM

The importance of commitment and mutuality was emphasized by Walton (1985) as follows: 'The new HRM model is composed of policies that promote mutuality – mutual goals, mutual influence, mutual respect, mutual rewards, mutual responsibility. The theory is that policies of mutuality will elicit commitment which in turn will yield both better economic performance and greater human development.'

David Guest (1987) wrote that one of the HRM policy goals was the achievement of high commitment – 'behavioural commitment to pursue agreed goals, and attitudinal commitment reflected in a strong identification with the enterprise'.

It was noted by Karen Legge (1995) that human resources 'may be tapped most effectively by mutually consistent policies that promote commitment and which, as a consequence, foster a willingness in employees to act flexibly in the interests of the "adaptive organization's" pursuit of excellence'.

But this emphasis on commitment has been criticized from the earliest days of HRM. Guest (1987) asked: 'commitment to what?', and Fowler (1987) has stated:

> At the heart of the concept is the complete identification of employees with the aims and values of the business – employee involvement but on the company's terms. Power, in the HRM system, remains very firmly in the hands of the employer. Is it really possible to claim full mutuality when at the end of the day the employer can decide unilaterally to close the company or sell it to someone else?

People as 'human capital'

The notion that people should be regarded as assets rather than variable costs, in other words treated as human capital, was originally advanced by Beer *et al* (1984). HRM philosophy, as mentioned by Karen Legge (1995), holds that 'human resources are valuable and a source of competitive advantage'. Armstrong and Baron (2002) stated that 'People and their collective skills, abilities and experience, coupled with their ability to deploy these in the interests of the employing organization, are now recognized as making a significant contribution to organizational success and as constituting a significant source of competitive advantage.'

Unitary philosophy

The HRM approach to employee relations is basically unitary – it is believed that employees share the same interests as employers. This contrasts with what could be regarded as the more realistic pluralist view, which says that all organizations contain a number of interest groups and that the interests of employers and employees do not necessarily coincide.

Individualistic

HRM is individualistic in that it emphasizes the importance of maintaining links between the organization and individual employees in preference to operating through group and representative systems.

HRM as a management-driven activity

HRM can be described as a central, senior management-driven strategic activity that is developed, owned and delivered by management as a whole to promote the interests of their organization. John Purcell (1993) thinks that 'the adoption of HRM is both a product of and a cause of a significant concentration of power in the hands of management', while the widespread use 'of the language of HRM, if not its practice, is a combination of its intuitive appeal to managers and, more importantly, a response to the turbulence of product and financial markets'. He asserts that HRM is about the rediscovery of management prerogative. He considers that HRM policies and practices, when applied within a firm as a break from the past, are often associated with words such as 'commitment', 'competence', 'empowerment', 'flexibility', 'culture', 'performance', 'assessment', 'reward', 'teamwork', 'involvement', 'cooperation', 'harmonization', 'quality' and 'learning'. But 'the danger of descriptions of HRM as modern best-management practice is that they stereotype the past and idealize the future'.

Keith Sisson (1990) suggests that 'The locus of responsibility for personnel management no longer resides with (or is "relegated to") specialist managers.' More recently, Purcell *et al* (2003) underline the importance of line management commitment and capability as the means by which HR policies are brought to life.

Focus on business values

The concept of HRM has been largely based on a management- and business-orientated philosophy. It is concerned with the total interests of the organization. The interests of the members of the organization are recognized but subordinated to those of the enterprise: hence the importance attached to strategic integration and strong cultures, which flow from top management's vision and leadership, and which require people who will be committed to the strategy, who will be adaptable to change and who will fit the culture. By implication, as Guest (1991) says, 'HRM is too important to be left to personnel managers.'

In 1995 Karen Legge noted that HRM policies are adapted to drive business values and are modified in the light of changing business objectives and conditions. She describes this process as 'thinking pragmatism' and suggests that evidence indicates more support for the hard versions of HRM than the soft version.

In accordance with labour process theory, Thompson and Harley (2007) believe that 'What is happening is a process of "capitalising on humanity" rather than investing in human capital.'

Recognizing the importance of moral and social values

The emphasis may be on the business case for HRM, but there is a growing body of opinion that there is more to HRM than that. Boxall *et al* (2007) stress that, 'While HRM does need to support commercial outcomes (often called "the business case"), it also exists to serve organizational needs for social legitimacy.' And it was noted by Paauwe (2004) that 'Added value represents the harsh world of economic rationality, but HRM is also about moral values... The yardstick of human resource outcomes is not just economic rationality – a stakeholder perspective is required, ie develop and maintain sustainable relationships with all the relevant stakeholders, not just customers and shareholders.'

Thomas Kochan (2007), Professor of Management at the MIT Sloan School of Management, believes that the HR profession 'has always had a special professional responsibility to balance the needs of the firm with the needs, aspirations and interests of the workforce and the values and standards society expects to be upheld at work... A regime which provides human beings no deep reason to care about one another cannot long preserve its legitimacy.'

RESERVATIONS ABOUT HRM

For some time, HRM was a controversial topic, especially in academic circles. The main reservations have been that HRM promises more than it delivers and that its morality is suspect.

HRM promises more than it can deliver

Noon (1992) has commented that HRM has serious deficiencies as a theory: 'It is built with concepts and propositions, but the associated variables and hypotheses are not made explicit. It is too comprehensive... If HRM is labelled a "theory" it raises expectations about its ability to describe and predict.'

Guest (1991) believes that HRM is an 'optimistic but ambiguous concept'; it is all hype and hope. Mabey *et al* (1998) follow this up by asserting that 'the heralded outcomes [of HRM] are almost without exception unrealistically high'. To put the concept of HRM into practice involves strategic integration, developing a coherent and consistent set of employment policies, and gaining commitment. This requires high levels of determination and competence at all levels of management and a strong and effective HR function staffed by business-orientated people. It may be difficult to meet these criteria, especially when the proposed HRM culture conflicts with the established corporate culture and traditional managerial attitudes and behaviour.

Gratton *et al* (1999) are convinced on the basis of their research that there is 'a disjunction between rhetoric and reality in the area of human resource management between HRM theory and HRM practice, between what the HR function says it is doing and that practice as perceived by employers, and between what senior management believes to be the role of the HR function, and the role it actually plays'. In their conclusions they refer to the 'hyperbole and rhetoric of human resource management'.

Caldwell (2004) believes that HRM 'is an unfinished project informed by a self-fulfilling vision of what it *should* be'.

The above comments are based on the assumption that there is a single monolithic form of HRM. This is not the case. HRM comes in all sorts of shapes and sizes. Sometimes it is just new wine in old bottles – personnel management under another name. Often it is aspirational, for example, in Walton's (1985) phrase, aiming to move 'from control to commitment'. It has to be conceded that many organizations that think they are practising HRM as described earlier are not doing so, at least to the full extent. It is difficult, and it is best not to expect too much. For example, most of the managements that hurriedly adopted performance-related pay as an HRM device that would act as a lever for change have been sorely disappointed.

However, the research conducted by Guest and Conway (1997) covering a stratified random sample of 1,000 workers established that a notably high level of HRM was found to be in place. This contradicts the view that management has tended to 'talk up' the adoption of HRM practices. The HRM characteristics covered by the survey included the opportunity to express grievances and raise personal concerns on such matters as opportunities for training and development, communications about business issues, single status, effective systems for dealing with bullying and harassment at work, making jobs interesting and varied, promotion from within, involvement programmes, no compulsory redundancies, performance-related pay, profit sharing and the use of attitude surveys.

The morality of HRM

HRM is accused by many academics of being manipulative if not positively immoral. Willmott (1993) remarks that HRM operates as a form of insidious 'control by compliance' when it emphasizes the need for employees to be committed to do what the organization wants them to do. It preaches mutuality but the reality is that behind the rhetoric it exploits workers. It is, they say, a wolf in sheep's clothing (Keenoy, 1990a). As Legge (1998) pointed out:

> Sadly, in a world of intensified competition and scarce resources, it seems inevitable that, as employees are used as means to an end, there will be some who will lose out. They may even be in the majority. For these people, the soft version of HRM may be an irrelevancy, while the hard version is likely to be an uncomfortable experience.

The accusation that HRM treats employees as means to an end is often made. However, it could be argued that, if organizations exist to achieve ends, which they obviously do, and if those ends can only be achieved through people, which is clearly the case, the concern of managements for commitment and performance from those people is not unnatural and is not attributable to the concept of HRM – it existed in the good old days of personnel management before HRM was invented. What matters is *how* managements treat people as ends and *what* managements provide in return.

Much of the hostility to HRM expressed by a number of academics is based on the belief that it is against the interests of workers, ie that it is managerialist. However, the Guest and Conway (1997) research established that the reports of workers on outcomes showed that a higher number of HR practices were associated with higher ratings of fairness, trust and management's delivery of their promises. Those experiencing more HR activities also felt more secure in and more satisfied with their jobs. Motivation was significantly higher for those working in organizations where more HR practices were in place. In summary, as commented by Guest (1999), it appears that workers like their experience of HRM. These findings appear to contradict the 'radical critique' view produced by academics such as Mabey *et al* (1998) that HRM has been ineffectual, pernicious (ie managerialist) or both. Some of those who adopt this stance tend to dismiss favourable reports from workers about HRM on the grounds that they have been brainwashed by management. But there is no evidence to support this view.

Moreover, as Armstrong (2000) points out:

HRM cannot be blamed or given credit for changes that were taking place anyway. For example, it is often alleged to have inspired a move from pluralism to unitarism in industrial relations. But newspaper production was moved from Fleet Street to Wapping by Murdoch, not because he had read a book about HRM but as a means of breaking the print unions' control.

Contradictions in the reservations about HRM

Guest (1999) has suggested that there are two contradictory concerns about HRM. The first as formulated by Legge (1995, 1998) is that, while management rhetoric may express concern for workers, the reality is harsher. And Keenoy (1997) complains that 'The real puzzle about HRMism is how, in the face of such apparently overwhelming critical "refutation", it has secured such influence and institutional presence.'

Other writers, however, simply claim that HRM does not work. Scott (1994), for example, finds that both management and workers are captives of their history and find it very difficult to let go of their traditional adversarial orientations.

But these contentions are contradictory. Guest (1999) remarks that 'It is difficult to treat HRM as a major threat (though what it is a threat to is not always made explicit) deserving of serious critical analysis while at the same time claiming that it is not practiced or is ineffective.'

2

The concept of strategy

Strategy was originally a military term, defined in the *Oxford English Dictionary* as: 'The art of a commander-in-chief; the art of projecting and directing the larger military movements and operations of a campaign.' Commanders-in-chief and military campaigns do not exist in business, the public sector or voluntary organizations, but at least this definition conveys the messages that strategy is the ultimate responsibility of the head of the organization, is an art and is concerned with projecting and directing large movements.

It was Peter Drucker who long ago (1955) pointed out in *The Practice of Management* the importance of strategic decisions, which he defined as 'all decisions on business objectives and on the means to reach them'.

However, the concept of business strategy was not fully developed until three outstanding pioneers, Kenneth Andrews (1987), Igor Ansoff (1987) and Alfred Chandler (1962) made their mark. They were followed by Michael Porter (1985), Henry Mintzberg (1987), Hamel and Prahalad (1989) and many more who further developed the concepts and adapted them to contemporary conditions.

This chapter focuses on business strategy. It provides a bridge between the basic concept of human resource management as covered in Chapter 1 and strategic human resource management as described in Chapter 3. One of the purposes of the chapter is to counter the belief that business strategy is a highly rational affair that provides a firm basis for HR strategy. Business strategy is in fact a far more intuitive, evolutionary and reactive process than most people believe. This is the reality of strategic HRM that must be borne in mind when dealing with this compelling but often elusive concept.

The chapter starts with definitions of strategy and goes on to describe the fundamentals of strategy in more detail. It concludes with a review of the process of strategy formulation.

STRATEGY DEFINED

Strategy has two fundamental meanings. First, it is forward looking. It is about deciding where you want to go and how you mean to get there. It is concerned with both ends and means. In this sense a strategy is a declaration of intent: 'This is what we want to do and this is how we intend to do it.' Strategies define longer-term goals, but they also cover how those goals will be attained. They guide purposeful action to deliver the required result. A good strategy is one that works, one that in Abell's (1993) phrase enables organizations to adapt by 'mastering the present and pre-empting the future'.

The second meaning of strategy is conveyed by the concept of strategic fit. The focus is upon the organization and the world around it. To maximize competitive advantage a firm must match its capabilities and resources to the opportunities available in the external environment. As Hofer and Schendel (1986) conclude, 'A critical aspect of top management's work today involves matching organizational competences (internal resources and skills) with the opportunities and risks created by environmental change in ways that will be both effective and efficient over the time such resources will be deployed.'

Strategy has been defined in other ways by the many writers on this subject. For example:

> Strategy is the determination of the basic long-term goals and objectives of an enterprise, and the adoption of courses of action and the allocation of resources necessary for carrying out these goals.
>
> (Chandler, 1962)

> Strategy is a set of fundamental or critical choices about the ends and means of a business.
>
> (Child, 1972)

> [Strategy involves] the constant search for ways in which the firm's unique resources can be redeployed in changing circumstances.
>
> (Rumelt, 1984)

Strategy is concerned with the long-term direction and scope of an organization. It is also crucially concerned with how the organization positions itself with regard to the environment and in particular to its competitors... It is concerned with establishing competitive advantage, ideally sustainable over time, not by technical manoeuvring, but by taking an overall long-term perspective.

(Faulkner and Johnson, 1992)

Strategy is the direction and scope of an organization over the longer term, which matches its resources to its changing environment, and in particular, to its markets, customers and clients to meet stakeholder expectations.

(Johnson and Scholes, 1993)

Strategy should be understood as a framework of critical ends and means.

(Boxall, 1996)

Business strategy is concerned with the match between the internal capabilities of the company and its external environment.

(Kay, 1999)

The emphasis (in strategy) is on focused actions that differentiate the firm from its competitors.

(Purcell, 1999)

Strategy, then, is a set of strategic choices, some of which may be formally planned. It is inevitable that much, if not most, of a firm's strategy emerges in a stream of action over time.

(Boxall and Purcell, 2003)

THE CONCEPT OF STRATEGY

The concept of strategy is based on a number of associated concepts: competitive advantage, resource-based strategy, distinctive capabilities, strategic intent, strategic capability, strategic management, strategic goals and strategic plans.

Competitive advantage

The concept of competitive advantage was formulated by Michael Porter (1985). Competitive advantage, Porter asserts, arises out of a firm creating value for its customers. To achieve it, firms select markets in which they can excel and present a moving target to their competitors by continually improving their position.

Porter emphasized the importance of *differentiation*, which consists of offering a product or service 'that is perceived industry-wise as being unique', and *focus* – seeing a particular buyer group or product market 'more effectively or efficiently than competitors who compete more broadly'. He then developed his well-known framework of three generic strategies, innovation, quality and cost leadership, that organizations can use to gain competitive advantage.

A distinction has been made by Barney (1991) between the competitive advantage that a firm presently enjoys but others will be able to copy, and sustained competitive advantage, which competitors cannot imitate. This leads to the concept of distinctive capabilities.

Distinctive capabilities

As Kay (1999) comments, 'The opportunity for companies to sustain competitive advantage is determined by their capabilities.' A distinctive capability or competence can be described as an important feature that in Quinn's (1980) phrase 'confers superiority on the organization'. Kay extends this definition by emphasizing that there is a difference between distinctive capabilities and reproducible capabilities. Distinctive capabilities are those characteristics that cannot be replicated by competitors or can only be imitated with great difficulty. Reproducible capabilities are those that can be bought or created by any company with reasonable management skills, diligence and financial resources. Most technical capabilities are reproducible.

Prahalad and Hamel (1990) argue that competitive advantage stems in the long term when a firm builds 'core competences' that are superior to those of its rivals and when it learns faster and applies its learning more effectively than its competitors.

Distinctive capabilities or core competences describe what the organization is specially or uniquely capable of doing. They are what the company does particularly well in comparison with its competitors. Key capabilities can exist in such areas as technology, innovation, marketing, delivering quality, and making good use of human and financial resources. If a company is aware of what its distinctive capabilities are, it can concentrate on using and developing them without diverting effort into less rewarding activities. It can be argued that the most distinctive capability of all is that represented by the knowledge, skills, expertise and commitment of the employees of the organization. This belief provides the basis for the philosophy of strategic human resource management and human capital management. Four criteria have been proposed by Barney (1991) for deciding whether a resource can be regarded as a distinctive capability or competency: value creation for the customer, rarity compared to the competition, non-imitability and non-substitutability.

The concept of distinctive capability forms the foundation of the resource-based approach to strategy as described later in this chapter.

Strategic intent

In its simplest form, strategy could be described as an expression of the intentions of the organization – what it means to do and how, as Wickens (1987) put it, the business means to 'get from here to there'. As defined by Hamel and Prahalad (1989), strategic intent refers to the expression of the leadership position the organization wants to attain and establishes a clear criterion on how progress towards its achievement will be measured. Strategic intent could be a very broad statement of vision or mission and/or it could more specifically spell out the goals and objectives to be attained over the longer term.

The strategic intent sequence has been defined by Miller and Dess (1996) as:

1.   a broad *vision* of what the organization should be;
2.   the organization's *mission*;
3.   specific *goals*, which are operationalized as:
4.   strategic *objectives*.

Strategic capability

Strategic capability is a concept that refers to the ability of an organization to develop and implement strategies that will achieve sustained competitive advantage. It is therefore about the capacity to select the most appropriate vision, to define realistic intentions, to match resources to opportunities and to prepare and implement strategic plans.

The strategic capability of an organization depends on the strategic capabilities of its managers. People who display high levels of strategic capability know where they are going and know how they are going to get there. They recognize that, although they must be successful now to succeed in the future, it is always necessary to create and sustain a sense of purpose and direction.

The resource-based view

The resource-based view of strategy is that the strategic capability of a firm depends on its resource capability. It is based on the ideas of Penrose (1959), who wrote that the firm is 'an administrative organization and a collection of productive resources'. It was expanded by Wernerfelt (1984), who explained that strategy 'is a balance between the exploitation of existing resources and the development of new ones'. Resource-based strategy theorists such as Barney (1991) argue that sustained competitive advantage stems from the acquisition and effective use of bundles of distinctive resources that competitors cannot imitate.

As Boxall (1996) comments, 'Competitive success does not come simply from making choices in the present; it stems from building up distinctive capabilities over significant periods of time.' Teece, Pisano and Shuen (1997) define 'dynamic capabilities' as 'the capacity of a firm to renew, augment and adapt its core competences over time'.

Strategic management

The purpose of strategic management has been expressed by Rosabeth Moss Kanter (1984) as being to 'elicit the present actions for the future' and become 'action vehicles – integrating and institutionalizing mechanisms for change'. Strategic management has been defined by Pearce and Robinson (1988) as follows: 'Strategic management is the set of decisions and actions resulting in the formulation and implementation of strategies designed to achieve the objectives of an organization.'

Strategic management has been described by Burns (1992) as being primarily concerned with:

▌ the full scope of an organization's activities, including corporate objectives and organizational boundaries;
▌ matching the activities of an organization to the environment in which it operates;
▌ ensuring that the internal structures, practices and procedures enable the organization to achieve its objectives;
▌ matching the activities of an organization to its resource capability, assessing the extent to which sufficient resources can be provided to take advantage of opportunities or to avoid threats in the organization's environment;
▌ acquiring, divesting and reallocating resources;
▌ translating the complex and dynamic set of external and internal variables that an organization faces into a structured set of clear future objectives that can then be implemented on a day-to-day basis.

The focus is on identifying the organization's mission and strategies, but attention is also given to the resource base required to make it succeed. Managers who think strategically will have a broad and long-term view of where they are going. But they will also be aware that they are responsible, first, for planning how to allocate resources to opportunities that contribute to the implementation of strategy and, second, for managing these opportunities in ways that will add value to the results achieved by the firm.

The process of strategic management is modelled in Figure 2.1. It involves defining the organization's mission, analysing the internal and external environment, exercising strategic choice (there is always choice), formulating corporate and functional strategies and goals, implementing strategies and monitoring and evaluating progress in achieving goals. But in practice it is not as simple and linear as that. Boxall and Purcell (2003) believe that

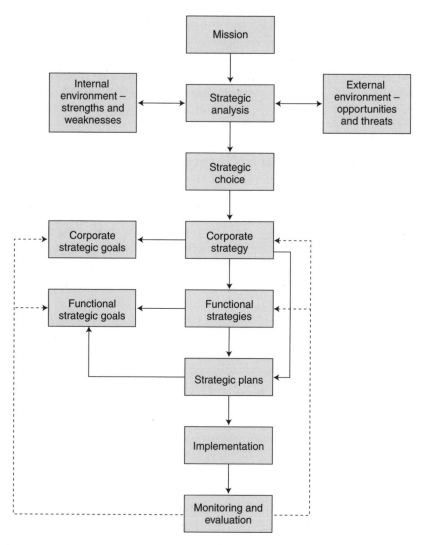

Figure 2.1   Strategic management model

strategic management 'is a mixed, impure, interactive process, fraught with difficulties, both intellectually and politically'.

Strategic goals

Strategic goals define where the organization wants to be. They may be specified in terms of actions, quantified in terms of growth, or expressed in general terms as aspirations rather than specifics.

Strategic plans

Strategic plans are formal expressions of how an organization intends to attain its strategic goals. Boxall and Purcell (2003) make the point that 'We should not make the mistake of equating the strategies of a firm with formal strategic plans... It is better if we understand the strategies of firms as *sets of strategic choices*, some of which may stem from planning exercises and set piece debates in senior management, and some of which emerge in a stream of action.'

THE FORMULATION OF STRATEGY

The formulation of corporate strategy is best described as a process for developing a sense of direction and ensuring strategic fit. It has often been described as a logical, step-by-step affair, the outcome of which is a formal written statement that provides a definitive guide to the organization's intentions. Many people still believe and act as if this were the case, but it is a misrepresentation of reality. This is not to dismiss completely the ideal of adopting a systematic approach as described below – it has its uses as a means of providing an analytical framework for strategic decision making and a reference point for monitoring the implementation of strategy. But in practice, and for reasons also explained below, the formulation of strategy can never be as rational and linear a process as some writers describe it or as some managers attempt to make it.

Approaches to strategy formulation

Whittington (1993) has identified four approaches to the formulation of strategy:

1. *Classical* – strategy formulation as a rational process of deliberate calculation. The process of strategy formulation is seen as being separate from the process of implementation.

2. *Evolutionary* – strategy formulation as an evolutionary process that is a product of market forces in which the most efficient and productive organizations win through.
3. *Processual* – strategy formulation as an incremental process that evolves through discussion and disagreement. It may be impossible to specify what the strategy is until after the event.
4. *Systemic* – strategy is shaped by the social system in which it is embedded. Choices are constrained by the cultural and institutional interests of a broader society rather than the limitations of those attempting to formulate corporate strategy.

The classical approach to formulating strategy

Conceptually, the classical approach as described by Whittington involves the following steps (implementation and monitoring steps have been added to the Whittington model):

1. Define the mission.
2. Set objectives.
3. Conduct internal and external environmental scans to assess internal strengths and weaknesses and external opportunities and threats (a SWOT analysis).
4. Analyse existing strategies to determine their relevance in the light of the internal and external appraisal. This may include gap analysis, which will establish the extent to which environmental factors might lead to gaps between what could be achieved if no changes were made and what needs to be achieved. The analysis will also cover resource capability, answering the question: 'Have we sufficient human or financial resources available now or that can readily be made available in the future to enable us to achieve our objectives?'
5. Define in the light of this analysis the distinctive capabilities of the organization.
6. Define the key strategic issues emerging from the previous analysis. These will be concerned with such matters as product-market scope, enhancing shareholder value and resource capability.
7. Determine corporate and functional strategies for achieving goals and competitive advantage, taking into account the key strategic issues. These may include business strategies for growth or diversification, or broad generic strategies for innovation, quality or cost leadership; or they could take the form of specific corporate/functional strategies concerned with product-market scope, technological development or human resource development.
8. Prepare integrated strategic plans for implementing strategies.

9. Implement the strategies.
10. Monitor implementation and revise existing strategies or develop new strategies as necessary.

This model of the process of strategy formulation should allow scope for iteration and feedback, and the activities incorporated in the model are all appropriate in any process of strategy formulation. But the model is essentially linear and deterministic – each step logically follows the earlier one and is conditioned entirely by the preceding sequence of events. This is not what happens in real life, where the formulation process is likely to correspond more closely to Whittington's evolutionary and 'processual' models.

The reality of strategy formulation

It has been said (Bower, 1982) that 'strategy is everything not well defined or understood'. This may be going too far but, in reality, strategy formulation can best be described as 'problem solving in unstructured situations' (Digman, 1990), and strategies will always be formed under conditions of partial ignorance.

The difficulty is that strategies are often based on the questionable assumption that the future will resemble the past. Some years ago, Robert Heller (1972) had a go at the cult of long-range planning: 'What goes wrong', he wrote, 'is that sensible anticipation gets converted into foolish numbers: and their validity always hinges on large loose assumptions.'

More recently, Faulkner and Johnson (1992) have said of long-range planning that it:

> was inclined to take a definitive view of the future, and to extrapolate trend lines for the key business variables in order to arrive at this view. Economic turbulence was insufficiently considered, and the reality that much strategy is formulated and implemented in the act of managing the enterprise was ignored. Precise forecasts ending with derived financials were constructed, the only weakness of which was that the future almost invariably turned out differently.

Strategy formulation is not necessarily a deterministic, rational and continuous process, as was pointed out by Mintzberg (1987). He believes that, rather than being consciously and systematically developed, strategy reorientation happens in what he calls brief 'quantum loops'. A strategy, according to Mintzberg, can be deliberate – it can realize the intentions of senior management, for example to attack and conquer a new market. But this is not always the case. In theory, he says, strategy is a systematic process: first we think and then we act; we formulate and then we implement. But we also 'act in order to think'. In practice, 'a realized strategy can emerge in response to an evolving situation', and the strategic planner is often 'a pattern organizer, a learner if you like, who manages a process in which strategies and visions can emerge as well as be deliberately conceived'. This concept of 'emergent strategy' conveys the essence of how in practice organizations develop their business and HR strategies.

Mintzberg was even more scathing about the weaknesses of strategic planning in his 1994 article in the *Harvard Business Review* on 'The rise and fall of strategic planning'. He contends that 'the failure of systematic planning is the failure of systems to do better than, or nearly as well as, human beings'. He went on to say that, 'Far from providing strategies, planning could not proceed without their prior existence... real strategists get their hands dirty digging for ideas, and real strategies are built from the nuggets they discover.' And 'sometimes strategies must be left as broad visions, not precisely articulated, to adapt to a changing environment'. He emphasized that strategic management is a *learning process* as managers of firms find out what works well in practice for them.

Other writers have criticized the deterministic concept of strategy. For example:

Business strategy, far from being a straightforward, rational phenomenon, is in fact interpreted by managers according to their own frame of reference, their particular motivations and information.

(Pettigrew and Whipp, 1991)

Although excellent for some purposes, the formal planning approach emphasizes 'measurable quantitative forces' at the expense of the 'qualitative, organizational and power-behavioural factors that so often determine strategic success'... Large organizations typically construct their strategies with processes which are 'fragmented, evolutionary, and largely intuitive'.

(Quinn, 1980)

The most effective decision-makers are usually creative, intuitive people 'employing an adaptive, flexible process'. Moreover, since most strategic decisions are event-driven rather than pre-programmed, they are unplanned.

(Digman, 1990)

Goold and Campbell (1986) also emphasize the variety and ambiguity of influences that shape strategy: 'Informed understandings work alongside more formal processes and analyses. The headquarters agenda becomes entwined with the business unit agenda, and both are interpreted in the light of personal interests. The sequence of events from decision to action can often be reversed, so that "decisions" get made retrospectively to justify actions that have already taken place.'

Mintzberg (1978, 1987, 1994) summarizes the non-deterministic view of strategy admirably. He perceives strategy as a 'pattern in a stream of activities' and highlights the importance of the interactive process between key players. He has emphasized the concept of 'emergent strategies', and a key aspect of this process is the production of something that is new to the organization even if this is not developed as logically as the traditional corporate planners believed was appropriate.

Kay (1999) also refers to the evolutionary nature of strategy. He comments that there is often little 'intentionality' in firms and that it is frequently the market rather than the visionary executive that chose the strategic match that was most effective. Quinn (1980) has produced the concept of 'logical incrementalism', which suggests that strategy evolves in several steps rather than being conceived as a whole.

The reality of strategic management

Tyson (1997) points out that, realistically, strategy:

∎ has always been emergent and flexible – it is always 'about to be' and it never exists at the present time;
∎ is not only realized by formal statements but also comes about by actions and reactions;
∎ is a description of a future-orientated action that is always directed towards change;
∎ is conditioned by the management process itself.

The reality of strategic management is that managers attempt to behave strategically in conditions of uncertainty, change and turbulence, even chaos. The phenomenon of bounded rationality as described by Miller *et al* (1999) applies – while people by their own lights are reasoned in their own behaviour, the reasoning behind their behaviour is influenced by 'human frailties and demands from both within and outside the organization'. The strategic management approach is as difficult as it is desirable, and this has to be borne in mind when consideration is given to the concept of strategic HRM as described in Chapter 3.

3

The concept of strategic human resource management

As Baird and Meshoulam (1988) remark: 'Business objectives are accomplished when human resource practices, procedures and systems are developed and implemented based on organizational needs, that is, when a strategic perspective to human resource management is adopted.' The aim of this chapter is to explore what this involves. It includes 1) a definition of strategic human resource management (strategic HRM), 2) an analysis of its underpinning concepts – the resource-based view and strategic fit, and 3) a description of how strategic HRM works, namely the universalistic, contingency and configurational perspectives defined by Delery and Doty (1996) and the three approaches associated with those perspectives – best practice, best fit and bundling. The chapter ends with discussions on the reality of strategic HRM and the practical implications of the theories reviewed earlier.

STRATEGIC HRM DEFINED

Strategic HRM is an approach that defines how the organization's goals will be achieved through people by means of HR strategies and integrated HR policies and practices.

Other definitions of strategic HRM include:

▮ Strategic HRM is concerned with 'seeing the people of the organization as a strategic resource for the achievement of competitive advantage' (Hendry and Pettigrew, 1986).
▮ 'A set of processes and activities jointly shared by human resources and line managers to solve people-related business problems' (Schuler and Walker, 1990).
▮ 'The macro-organizational approach to viewing the role and function of HRM in the larger organization' (Butler *et al*, 1991).
▮ 'The pattern of planned human resource deployments and activities intended to enable an organization to achieve its goals' (Wright and McMahan, 1992).
▮ 'Strategic HRM focuses on actions that differentiate the firm from its competitors' (Purcell, 1999).
▮ 'The central premise of strategic human resource management theory is that successful organizational performance depends on a close fit or alignment between business and human resource strategy' (Batt, 2007).

BASIS OF STRATEGIC HRM

Strategic HRM is based on three propositions:

1. The human resources or human capital of an organization play a strategic role in its success and are a major source of competitive advantage.
2. HR strategies should be integrated with business plans (*vertical integration*). As Allen and White (2007) stress, 'The central premise of strategic human resource management theory is that successful organizational performance depends on a close fit or alignment between business and human resource strategy.' Boxall *et al* (2007) also believe that 'The major focus of strategic HRM should be aligning HR with firm strategies.'
3. Individual HR strategies should cohere by being linked to each other to provide mutual support (*horizontal integration*).

Strategic HRM can be regarded as a mindset underpinned by certain concepts rather than a set of techniques. It provides the foundation for strategic reviews in which analysis of the organizational context and existing HR practices leads to choices on strategic plans for the development of overall or specific HR strategies (see Chapter 4). But strategic HRM is not just about strategic planning; it is also concerned with the implementation of strategy and the strategic behaviour of HR specialists working with their line management colleagues on an everyday basis to ensure that the business goals of the organization are achieved and its values are put into practice. The strategic role of HR professionals is examined in Chapter 5.

PRINCIPLES OF STRATEGIC HRM

Strategic HRM supplies a perspective on the way in which critical issues or success factors related to people can be addressed, and strategic decisions are made that have a major and long-term impact on the behaviour and success of the organization. It is not just concerned with 'mirroring current conditions or past practices' (Smith, 1982). As a means of developing integrated HR strategies, strategic HRM is facilitated to the extent to which the following seven principles set out by Ondrack and Nininger (1984) are followed:

1. There is an overall purpose and the human resource dimensions of that purpose are evident.
2. A process of developing strategy within the organization exists and is understood, and there is explicit consideration of human resource dimensions.
3. Effective linkages exist on a continuing basis to ensure the integration of human resource considerations with the organizational decision-making process.
4. The office of the chief executive provides the challenge for integrating human resource considerations to meet the needs of the business.
5. The organization of all levels establishes responsibility and accountability for human resource management.
6. Initiatives in the management of human resources are relevant to the needs of the business.
7. It includes the responsibility to identify and interact in the social, political, technological and economic environments in which the organization is and will be doing business.

AIMS OF STRATEGIC HRM

The fundamental aim of strategic HRM is to generate strategic capability by ensuring that the organization has the skilled, engaged and well-motivated employees it needs to achieve sustained competitive advantage. In accordance with the resource-based view as described later, the strategic goal will be to 'create firms which are more intelligent and flexible than their competitors' (Boxall, 1996) by hiring and developing more talented staff and by extending their skills base.

Schuler (1992) states that:

> Strategic human resource management is largely about integration and adaptation. Its concern is to ensure that: (1) human resources (HR) management is fully integrated with the strategy and strategic needs of the firm; (2) HR policies cohere both across policy areas and across hierarchies; and (3) HR practices are adjusted, accepted and used by line managers and employees as part of their everyday work.

As Dyer and Holder (1988) remark, strategic HRM provides 'unifying frameworks which are at once broad, contingency based and integrative'. The rationale for strategic HRM is the perceived advantage of having an agreed and understood basis for developing and implementing approaches to people management that take into account the changing context in which the firm operates and its longer-term requirements. It has been suggested by Lengnick-Hall and Lengnick-Hall (1988, 1990) that underlying this rationale in a business is the concept of achieving competitive advantage through HRM.

When considering the aims of strategic HRM it is necessary to address the issue of the extent to which HR strategy should take into account ethical considerations – the interests of all the stakeholders in the organization and employees in general, as well as owners and management and the responsibilities of the organization to the wider community.

In Storey's (1989) terms 'soft strategic HRM' will place greater emphasis on the human-relations aspect of people management, stressing continuous development, communication, involvement, security of employment, the quality of working life and work–life balance. 'Hard strategic HRM' on the other hand will emphasize the yield to be obtained by investing in human resources in the interests of the business. Strategic HRM should attempt to achieve a proper balance between the hard and soft elements. All organizations exist to achieve a purpose, and they must ensure that they have the resources required to do so and that they use them effectively. But they should also take into account the human factors contained in the concept of soft strategic HRM. In the words of Quinn Mills (1983) they should plan with people in mind, taking into account the needs and aspirations of all the members of the organization. The problem is that hard considerations in many businesses will come first, leaving soft ones some way behind.

Organizations must also consider their responsibilities to society in general on the grounds that because they draw resources from society they must give back to society. The exercise of corporate social responsibility, defined by McWilliams, Siegel and Wright (2006) as 'actions that appear to further some social good beyond the interests of the firm and that which is required by law', may be regarded as outside the scope of human resource management. But because it relates to ethical actions in the interests of people there is a strong link, and it is therefore an aspect of organizational behaviour that can legitimately be included in the strategic portfolio of HR specialists.

CONCEPTS OF STRATEGIC HRM

Strategic HRM is underpinned by three concepts, namely the resource-based view, strategic fit and strategic flexibility.

The resource-based view

To a large extent, the philosophy of strategic HRM is based on the resource-based view. This states that it is the range of resources in an organization, including its human resources, that produces its unique character and creates competitive advantage (Hamel and Prahalad, 1989). The resource-based view as developed by Penrose (1959) and expanded by Wernerfelt (1984) provides 'a durable basis for strategy' (Grant, 1991) and 'builds on and provides a unifying framework for the field of strategic human resource management' (Kamoche, 1996).

Jay Barney (1991, 1995) states that competitive advantage arises first when firms within an industry are heterogeneous with respect to the strategic resources they control and, second, when these resources are not perfectly mobile across firms and thus heterogeneity can be long-lasting. Creating sustained competitive advantage therefore depends on the unique resources and capabilities that a firm brings to competition in its environment. These resources include all the experience, knowledge, judgement, risk-taking propensity and wisdom of individuals associated with a firm. For a firm resource to have the potential for creating sustained competitive advantage it should have four attributes: it must be 1) valuable, 2) rare, 3) imperfectly imitable and 4) non-substitutable. To discover these resources and capabilities, managers must look inside their firm for valuable, rare and costly-to-imitate resources, and then exploit these resources through their organization.

Wright and McMahan (1992) also argue that competitive advantage through people resources arises because 1) there is heterogeneity in their availability in the sense of the differences that exist between them across firms in an industry and 2) they are immobile in the sense that competing firms may be unable to recruit them. They follow Barney (1991) in listing four criteria that govern the ability of a resource to provide sustained competitive advantage, namely 1) the resource must add positive value to the firm, 2) the resource must be unique or rare among current and potential competitors, 3) the resource must be imperfectly imitable, and 4) the resource cannot be substituted with another resource by competing firms.

Resource-based strategic HRM can produce what Boxall and Purcell (2003) refer to as human resource advantage. The aim is to develop strategic capability. This means strategic fit between resources and opportunities, obtaining added value from the effective deployment of resources, and developing people who can think and plan strategically in the sense that they understand the key strategic issues and ensure that what they do supports the achievement of the business's strategic goals.

The significance of the resource-based view of the firm is that it highlights the importance of a human capital management approach to HRM and provides the justification for investing in people through resourcing, talent management and learning and development programmes as a means of enhancing competitive advantage.

Strategic fit

As explained by Wright and McMahan (1992) strategic fit refers to the two dimensions that distinguish strategic HRM: 'First, vertically, it entails the linking of human resource management practices with the strategic management processes of the organization. Second, horizontally, it empha-sizes the coordination or congruence among the various human resource management practices.'

Strategic flexibility

Strategic flexibility is defined as the ability of the firm to respond and adapt to changes in its competitive environment. Environmental differences will affect a flexibility strategy. As indicated by Wright and Snell (1998), in a stable, predictable environment the strategy could be to develop people with a narrow range of skills (or not to develop multiskilled people) and to elicit a narrow range of behaviour (eg tight job descriptions). In a dynamic, unpre-dictable environment, however, organizations might develop organic HR systems that produce a human capital pool with people possessing a wide range of skills who can engage in a wide variety of behaviours. The need is to achieve resource flexibility by developing a variety of 'behavioural scripts' and encourage employees to apply them in different situations, bearing in mind the increased amount of discretionary behaviour that may be appro-priate in different roles.

It can be argued that the concepts of strategic flexibility and fit are incompatible: 'fit' implies a fixed relationship between the HR strategy and business strategy, but the latter has got to be flexible, so how can good fit be maintained? But Wright and Snell have suggested that the concepts of fit and flexibility are complementary – fit exists at a point in time, while flexibility has to exist over a period of time.

PERSPECTIVES ON STRATEGIC HRM

Taking into account the concepts of the resource-based view and strategic fit, Delery and Doty (1996) contend that 'organizations adopting a particular strategy require HR practices that are different from those required by organizations adopting different strategies' and that organizations with 'greater congruence between their HR strategies and their [business] strategies should enjoy superior performance'. They identify three HRM perspectives:

1. *The universalistic perspective* – some HR practices are better than others and all organizations should adopt these best practices. There is a universal relationship between individual 'best' practices and firm performance.
2. *The contingency perspective* – in order to be effective, an organization's HR policies must be consistent with other aspects of the organization. The primary contingency factor is the organization's strategy. This can be described as 'vertical fit'.
3. *The configurational perspective* – this is a holistic approach that emphasizes the importance of the *pattern* of HR practices and is concerned with how this pattern of independent variables is related to the dependent variable of organizational performance. Organizational configuration has been defined by Meyer *et al* (1993) as 'any multi-dimensional constellation of conceptually distinct characteristics that commonly occur together... [which] may be represented in typologies'. Delery and Doty (1996) refer to the Miles and Snow (1978) typology, which defines three ideal strategic types of organizations – the prospector, the analyser and the defender – as a configurational concept, and also mention MacDuffie's (1995) research, which identified specific configurations or 'bundles' that enhance firm performance. Confusingly, configuration as described by Delery and Doty appears to have two meanings: 1) the degree of fit between a total HR system and an organizational type, eg the ideal types of Miles and Snow; and 2) the extent to which HR practices are linked together into a total system.

A way of resolving this confusion was suggested by Richardson and Thompson (1999). They proposed adopting the commonly used terms of best-practice and best-fit approaches for the universalistic and contingency perspectives and 'bundling' as the third approach. This followed the classification made by Guest (1997) of fit as an ideal set of practices, fit as contingency and fit as bundles. The implication of this classification is that the configurational perspective of Delery and Doty referring to fit between the HR system and an organizational type should be included under the heading of 'best fit', while their reference to linking HR practices in a total system should be treated separately under the heading of 'bundling'. The best-practice, best-fit and bundling approaches are discussed below.

THE BEST-PRACTICE APPROACH

This approach is based on the assumption that there is a set of best HRM practices and that adopting them will inevitably lead to superior organizational performance. They are universal in the sense that they are best in any situation.

Lists of best practices

A number of lists of 'best practices' have been produced, the best known of which was produced by Pfeffer (1994), namely:

1. employment security;
2. selective hiring;
3. self-managed teams;
4. high compensation contingent on performance;
5. training to provide a skilled and motivated workforce;
6. reduction of status differentials;
7. sharing information.

The following list was drawn up by Guest (1999):

1. selection and the careful use of selection tests to identify those with potential to make a contribution;
2. training, and in particular a recognition that training is an ongoing activity;
3. job design to ensure flexibility, commitment and motivation, including steps to ensure that employees have the responsibility and autonomy fully to use their knowledge and skills;
4. communication to ensure that a two-way process keeps everyone fully informed;

5. employee share ownership programmes to increase employees' awareness of the implications of their actions on the financial performance of the firm.

Delery and Doty (1996) identified seven strategic HR practices, ie ones that are related to overall organizational performance: the use of internal career ladders, formal training systems, results-orientated appraisal, performance-based compensation, employment security, employee voice and broadly defined jobs.

High-performance work systems as described in Chapter 9 can incorporate best-practice characteristics, eg the US Department of Labor (1993), Appelbaum *et al* (2000), Sung and Ashton (2005) and Thompson and Heron (2005). Another list for high-commitment practices was produced by Wood and Albanese (1995).

Problems with the best-practice model

The 'best practice' rubric has been attacked by a number of commentators. Cappelli and Crocker-Hefter (1996) comment that the notion of a single set of best practices has been overstated: 'There are examples in virtually every industry of firms that have very distinctive management practices... Distinctive human resource practices shape the core competencies that determine how firms compete.'

Purcell (1999) has also criticized the best-practice or universalist view by pointing out the inconsistency between a belief in best practice and the resource-based view, which focuses on the intangible assets, including HR, that allow the firm to do better than its competitors. He asks how can 'the universalism of best practice be squared with the view that only some resources and routines are important and valuable by being rare and imperfectly imitable?'

In accordance with contingency theory, which emphasizes the importance of interactions between organizations and their environments so that what organizations do is dependent on the context in which they operate, it is difficult to accept that there is any such thing as universal best practice. What works well in one organization will not necessarily work well in another because it may not fit its strategy, culture, management style, technology or working practices. As Becker *et al* (1997) remark: 'Organizational high-performance work systems are highly idiosyncratic and must be tailored carefully to each firm's individual situation to achieve optimum results.'

However, a knowledge of what is assumed to be best practice can be used to inform decisions on what practices are most likely to fit the needs of the organization, as long as it is understood *why* a particular practice should be regarded as a best practice and what needs to be done to ensure that it will work in the context of the organization. Becker and Gerhart (1996) argue that the idea of best practice might be more appropriate for identifying the principles underlying the choice of practices, as opposed to the practices themselves. Perhaps it is best to think of 'good practice' rather than 'best practice'.

THE BEST-FIT APPROACH

The best-fit approach emphasizes that HR strategies should be contingent on the context, circumstances of the organization and its type. 'Best fit' can be perceived in terms of vertical integration or alignment between the organization's business and HR strategies. There is a choice of models, namely life cycle, competitive strategy, and strategic configuration.

The life cycle model

The life cycle model is based on the theory that the development of a firm takes place in four stages: start-up, growth, maturity and decline. This is in line with product life cycle theory.

The basic premise of this model was expressed by Baird and Meshoulam (1988) as follows: 'Human resource management's effectiveness depends on its fit with the organization's stage of development. As the organization grows and develops, human resource management programmes, practices and procedures must change to meet its needs. Consistent with growth and development models it can be suggested that human resource management develops through a series of stages as the organization becomes more complex.'

As Buller and Napier (1993) explain, in a start-up phase, management of the HR function may be loose and informal; it may even be performed by the founder/owner. As the organization experiences high growth in sales, products and markets, the demand for new employees increases. This demand is beyond the capacity of the founder and line managers to handle. The organization typically responds to this pressure by adding more formal structure and functional specialists, including HR. The role of HR in this high-growth stage is to attract the right kinds and numbers of people, but it is also the time for innovation and the development of talent management, performance management, learning and development and reward policies and practices. As the organization matures, HR may become less innovative and more inclined to consolidate and develop existing practices rather than create new ones. In the decline stage HR may not have the scope to engage so wholeheartedly with the programmes operating in maturity. HR might well be involved in the difficult decisions that follow downsizing and being taken over.

This is a plausible picture of what may happen, and it is backed up by some empirical research; for example, a study by Schuler and Jackson (1987) found evidence that firms with products in the growth stage placed higher priorities on HR management innovation and planning than firms with products in the mature phase. But it is a model of what might happen rather than what should happen. There seems to be no good reason why the HR function in a mature firm should rest on its laurels: quite the opposite. Perhaps the model can serve most usefully as an analytical tool that can be used to alert HR planners to what is happening in the firm.

Best fit and competitive strategies

Three strategies aimed at achieving competitive advantage have been identified by Porter (1985):

1. *innovation* – being the unique producer;
2. *quality* – delivering high-quality goods and services to customers;
3. *cost leadership* – the planned result of policies aimed at 'managing away' expense.

Schuler and Jackson (1987) claim on the basis of their research that 'effectiveness can be increased by systematically melding human resource practices with the selected competitive strategy'. They described the HR characteristics of firms pursuing one or other of the three strategies (Table 3.1).

Strategic configuration

Another approach to best fit is the proposition that organizations will be more effective if they adopt a policy of strategic configuration (Delery and Doty, 1996) by matching their strategy to one of the ideal types defined by theories such as those produced by Mintzberg (1979) and Miles and Snow (1978). This increased effectiveness is attributed to the internal consistency or fit between the patterns of relevant contextual, structural and strategic factors.

The typology of organizations produced by Mintzberg (1979) classified them into five ideal types: simple structure, machine bureaucracy, professional bureaucracy, divisionalized form and adhocracy.

Miles and Snow (1978) identified four types of organizations, classifying the first three types as 'ideal' organizations:

1. *Prospectors*, which operate in an environment characterized by rapid and unpredictable changes. They react to this environment by focusing on

Table 3.1 Fitting HR characteristics to competitive strategies

Innovation Strategy	Quality Strategy	Cost Leadership Strategy
Jobs that require close interaction and coordination among groups of individuals.	Relatively fixed and explicit job descriptions.	Relatively fixed and explicit job descriptions.
Performance appraisals that are more likely to reflect longer-term and group-based achievements.	High levels of employee participation.	Narrowly designed jobs and career paths that encourage specialization. Short-term and results-oriented appraisals.
Jobs that allow employees to develop skills that can be used in other positions in the firm.	A mix of group and individual criteria for appraisal that is mostly short-term and results-oriented.	Close monitoring of market pay levels for use in making compensation decisions.
Compensation systems that emphasize internal equity rather than external or market-based equity.	Relative egalitarian treatment of employees and some guarantees of employee security.	Minimal levels of employee training and development.
Pay rates that tend to be low but allow employees to be stockholders and have more freedom to choose the mix of components.	Extensive and continuous training and development of employees.	Practices that maximize efficiency by providing means for management to monitor and control closely the activities of employees.
Broad career paths to reinforce the development of a wide range of skills.		

Source: Schuler and Jackson (1987)

the development of new products, markets and technologies. They create change in their markets and are the forces to which competitors must respond. Prospectors have low levels of formalization and specialization and high levels of decentralization. They have relatively few hierarchical levels.

2. *Defenders*, which operate in a more stable and predictable environment than prospectors and engage in more long-term planning. Their emphasis is on defending their markets, and they do little research and development. Defenders focus on efficiency by relying on routine technologies and economies of scale. They have more mechanistic or bureaucratic structures than prospectors and obtain coordination through formalization, centralization, specialization and vertical differentiation.

3.   *Analysers*, which are a combination of the prospector and defender types. They operate in stable environments like defenders and also in markets where new products are constantly required like prospectors. They are usually not the initiators of change like prospectors but they follow the changes more rapidly than defenders. Analysers seek effectiveness through both efficiency and new products or markets. This dual focus may result in increased size, because analysers must engage in both mass production and research and development. They are usually not the initiators of change, as are prospectors, but they follow the changes more rapidly than defenders. They may also exhibit higher levels of interdependence than either prospectors or defenders.

4.   *Reactors*, which are unstable organizations existing in what they believe to be an unpredictable environment. They lack consistent, well-articulated strategies and do not undertake long-range planning.

Delery and Doty (1996) suggest that organizations should align their HR systems with the strategy linked to their configuration. Two systems are identified. In the *market-type system* hiring is mainly from outside the organization, little use is made of internal career ladders, there is no formal training, performance appraisal is results-orientated, there is not much security, and jobs are not clearly defined. In the *internal system* hiring is mainly from within the organization, extensive use is made of career ladders, a lot of formal training is provided, performance is appraised by behaviour-orientated measures, there is considerable security, and jobs are tightly defined. The prospector strategy requires a market system, while the internal system is appropriate for the defender strategy. Delery and Doty make no suggestions on what is appropriate for the analyser strategy, but presumably this leads to some form of hybrid market/internal HR system.

Research conducted by Doty *et al* (1993) established that the Miles and Snow theory had a high level of predictive validity. In other words, it indicated a reasonably powerful link between fit, in terms of context, structure and strategy, and organizational effectiveness. However, they did remark, rather obscurely, that: 'Multicollinearity may have contributed to instability in the canonical variates.' The same research failed to establish any significant link between organizational effectiveness and the Mintzberg typology.

Comments on the concept of best fit

The best-fit model seems to be more realistic than the best-practice model. As Dyer and Holder (1988) point out, 'The inescapable conclusion is that what is best depends.' It can therefore be claimed that best fit is more important than best practice. But there are limitations to the concept of best fit. Paauwe

(2004) emphasizes that 'It is necessary to avoid falling into the trap of "contingent determinism" (ie claiming that the context determines the strategy). There is, or should be, room for making strategic choices.'

There is a danger of mechanistically matching HR polices and practices with strategy. It is not credible to claim that there are single contextual factors that determine HR strategy, and internal fit cannot therefore be complete. As Boxall *et al* (2007) point out, 'It is clearly impossible to make *all* HR policies reflective of a chosen competitive or economic mission; they may have to fit with social legitimacy goals.' And Purcell (1999) comments that 'The search for a contingency or matching model of HRM is also limited by the impossibility of modelling all the contingent variables, the difficulty of showing their interconnection, and the way in which changes in one variable have an impact on others.'

Best-fit models tend to be static and don't take account of the processes of change. They neglect the fact that institutional forces shape HRM – it cannot be assumed that employers are free agents able to make independent decisions.

The problem of assuming that classifications provide causal explanations was summed up in the remark made by Alice to the Red Queen: 'Naming something is not the same as explaining it.'

BUNDLING

As Richardson and Thompson (1999) comment, 'A strategy's success turns on combining "vertical" or external fit and "horizontal" or internal fit.' They conclude that a firm with bundles of associated HR practices should have a higher level of performance, providing it also achieves high levels of fit with its competitive strategy.

'Bundling' is the development and implementation of several HR practices together so that they are interrelated and therefore complement and reinforce each other. This is the process of horizontal integration, which is also referred to as the use of 'complementarities'. MacDuffie (1995) explained the concept of bundling as follows: 'Implicit in the notion of a "bundle" is the idea that practices within bundles are interrelated and internally consistent, and that "more is better" with respect to the impact on performance, because of the overlapping and mutually reinforcing effect of multiple practices.'

The aim of bundling is to achieve high performance through coherence, which is one of the four 'meanings' of strategic HRM defined by Hendry and Pettigrew (1986). Coherence exists when a mutually reinforcing set of HR policies and practices have been developed that jointly contribute to the attainment of the organization's strategies for matching resources to organizational needs, improving performance and quality and, in commercial enterprises, achieving competitive advantage.

The process of bundling HR strategies is an important aspect of the concept of strategic HRM. In a sense, strategic HRM is holistic; it is concerned with the organization as a total system and addresses what needs to be done across the organization as a whole. It is not interested in isolated programmes and techniques, or in the ad hoc development of HR practices.

Dyer and Reeves (1995) note that 'The logic in favour of bundling is straightforward... Since employee performance is a function of both ability and motivation, it makes sense to have practices aimed at enhancing both.' Thus there are several ways in which employees can acquire needed skills (such as careful selection and training) and multiple incentives to enhance motivation (different forms of financial and non-financial rewards). Their study of various models listing HR practices that create a link between HRM and business performance found that the activities appearing in most of the models were involvement, careful selection, extensive training and contingent compensation.

On the basis of his research in flexible production manufacturing plants in the United States, MacDuffie (1995) noted that flexible production gives employees a much more central role in the production system. They have to resolve problems as they appear on the line, and this means that they have to possess both a conceptual grasp of the production process and the analytical skills to identify the root cause of problems. But the multiple skills and conceptual knowledge developed by the workforce in flexible production firms are of little use unless workers are motivated to contribute mental as well as physical effort. Such discretionary effort on problem solving will only be contributed if workers 'believe that their individual interests are aligned with those of the company, and that the company will make a reciprocal investment in their wellbeing'. This means that flexible production techniques have to be supported by bundles of high-commitment human resource practices such as employment security, pay that is partly contingent on performance, and a reduction of status barriers between managers and workers. Company investment in building worker skills also contributes to this 'psychological contract of reciprocal commitment'. The research indicated that plants using flexible production systems, which bundle human resource practices into a system that is integrated with production/business strategy, outperform plants using more traditional mass production systems in both productivity and quality.

Following research in 43 automobile processing plants in the United States, Pil and MacDuffie (1996) established that, when a high-involvement work practice is introduced in the presence of complementary HR practices, not only does the new work practice produce an incremental improvement in performance but so do the complementary practices.

One way of looking at the concept is to say that coherence will be achieved if there is an overriding strategic imperative or driving force, such as high performance, customer service, quality, talent management or the need to develop skills and competences, that initiates various processes and policies designed to link together and operate in concert to deliver results.

Specifically, bundling can take place in a number of other ways. For example, the development of high-performance, high-commitment or high-involvement systems (see Chapters 4 and 9) is in effect bundling because it groups a number of HR practices together to produce synergy and thus make a greater impact. Another form of bundling is provided by competency frameworks, which are used in assessment and development centres and to specify recruitment standards, identify learning and development needs, indicate the standards of behaviour or performance required and serve as the basis for human resource planning. They could also be incorporated into performance management processes in which the aims are primarily developmental and competencies are used as criteria for reviewing behaviour and assessing learning and development needs. Job evaluation could be based on levels of competency, and competency-based pay systems could be introduced. Grade structures can define career ladders in terms of competency requirements (career family structures) and thus provide the basis for learning and development programmes. They can serve the dual purpose of defining career paths and pay progression opportunities.

The problem with the bundling approach is that of deciding what is the best way to relate different practices together. There is no evidence that one bundle is generally better than another.

THE REALITY OF STRATEGIC HRM

Strategic HRM, as this chapter has shown, has been a happy hunting ground for academics over many years. But what does all this conceptualizing mean in real life? What can practitioners learn from it as they go about their business?

Before answering these questions it is worth recalling the rationale for strategic HRM, which is that it is the basis for developing and implementing approaches to people management that take into account the changing context in which the firm operates and its longer-term requirements. It should also be borne in mind that strategic HRM is a mindset, which only becomes real when it produces actions and reactions that can be regarded as strategic, in the form of either overall or specific HR strategies or strategic behaviour on the part of HR professionals working alongside line managers.

As modelled in Figure 3.1 strategic HRM is about both HR strategies and the strategic management activities of HR professionals. There is always choice about those strategies and the strategic role of HR, and this choice is based on strategic analysis as conducted in strategic reviews.

PRACTICAL IMPLICATIONS OF STRATEGIC HRM THEORY

It was famously remarked by Douglas McGregor (1960) that there is nothing so practical as a good theory, ie one that is the product of rigorous field research and, probably, tested by further research. This is certainly the case with strategic HR theory, which is based on thorough research and testing and, once the jargon has been discarded, has a strong common-sense appeal.

The theory addresses major people issues that affect or are affected by the strategic plans of the organization, provides a rationale for having an agreed and understood basis for developing and implementing approaches to people management that take into account the changing context in which the firm operates and its longer-term requirements, and ensures that business and HR strategy and functional HR strategies are aligned with one another. It demonstrates that:

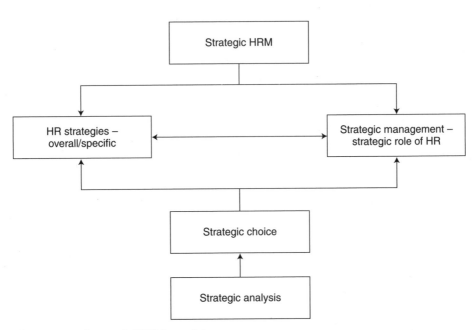

Figure 3.1   Strategic HRM model

- creating sustained competitive advantage depends on the unique resources and capabilities that a firm brings to competition in its environment (Baron, 2001);
- competitive advantage is achieved by ensuring that the firm has higher-quality people than its competitors (Purcell *et al*, 2003);
- the competitive advantage based on the effective management of people is hard to imitate (Barney, 1991);
- the challenge to organizations is to ensure that they have the capability to find, assimilate, compensate and retain the talented individuals they need (Ulrich, 1998);
- it is unwise to pursue so-called 'best practice' (the 'universalistic' perspective of Delery and Doty, 1996) without being certain that what happens elsewhere would work in the context of the organization;
- 'best fit' (the 'contingency' perspective of Delery and Doty, 1996) is preferable to 'best practice' as long as the organization avoids falling into the trap of 'contingent determinism' by allowing the context to determine the strategy (Paauwe, 2004);
- the search for best fit is limited by the impossibility of modelling all the contingent variables, the difficulty of showing their interconnection, and the way in which changes in one variable have an impact on others (Purcell, 1999);
- best fit can be pursued in a number of ways, namely by fitting the HR strategy to its position in its life cycle of start-up, growth, maturity or decline (Baird and Meshoulam, 1988), or the competitive strategy of innovation, quality or cost leadership (Porter, 1985), or the organization's 'strategic configuration' (Delery and Doty, 1996), eg the typology of organizations as prospectors, defenders and analysers defined by Miles and Snow (1978);
- improved performance can be achieved by 'bundling', ie the development and implementation of several HR practices together so that they are interrelated and therefore complement and reinforce each other (MacDuffie, 1995).

Part 2

The practice of strategic HRM

4

HR strategies

As described in Chapter 3 strategic HRM is a mindset, which leads to strategic actions and reactions, in the form of either overall or specific HR strategies or strategic behaviour on the part of HR professionals. The role of HR is covered in Chapter 5. This chapter focuses on HR strategies under the following headings:

▌ What are HR strategies?
▌ What is the purpose of HR strategies?
▌ What are the main types of overall HR strategies?
▌ What are the main areas in which specific HR strategies are developed?
▌ What are the criteria for an effective HR strategy?
▌ How should HR strategies be developed?
▌ How should HR strategies be implemented?

Part 4 of this book contains a strategic HRM toolkit, which provides guidance on conducting a strategic review as the basis or the development of HR strategies.

WHAT ARE HR STRATEGIES?

HR strategies set out what the organization intends to do about its human resource management policies and practices and how they should be integrated with the business strategy and each other. They are described by Dyer and Reeves (1995) as 'internally consistent bundles of human resource practices', and in the words of Peter Boxall (1996) they provide 'a framework of critical ends and means'. Richardson and Thompson (1999) suggest that 'A strategy, whether it is an HR strategy or any other kind of management strategy, must have two key elements: there must be strategic objectives (ie things the strategy is supposed to achieve), and there must be a plan of action (ie the means by which it is proposed that the objectives will be met).'

Because all organizations are different, all HR strategies are different. There is no such thing as a standard strategy, and research into HR strategy conducted by Armstrong and Long (1994) and Armstrong and Baron (2002) revealed many variations. Some strategies are simply very general declarations of intent. Others go into much more detail. But two basic types of HR strategies can be identified. These are: 1) overall strategies such as high-performance working; and 2) specific strategies relating to the different aspects of human resource management such as learning and development and reward.

WHAT IS THE PURPOSE OF HR STRATEGIES?

The purpose of HR strategies is to articulate what an organization intends to do about its human resource management policies and practices now and in the longer term, bearing in mind the dictum of Fombrun *et al* (1984) that business and managers should perform well in the present to succeed in the future. HR strategies may set out intentions and provide a sense of purpose and direction, but they are not just long-term plans. As Lynda Gratton (2000) commented, 'There is no great strategy, only great execution.'

OVERALL HR STRATEGIES

Overall strategies describe the general intentions of the organization about how people should be managed and developed and what steps should be taken to ensure that the organization can attract and retain the people it needs and ensure so far as possible that employees are committed, motivated and engaged. There are four categories of overall strategy:

1. An emergent, evolutionary and possibly unarticulated understanding of the required approach to human resource management. This will be influenced by the business strategy as it develops, the position of the

organization in its life cycle, and the organizational configuration (prospector, defender or analyser). It will also be affected by the views, experience and management style of the chief executive, senior managers and the head of HR, whose influence will depend on position and credibility.

2. Broad-brush statements of aims and purpose that set the scene for more specific strategies. They will be concerned with overall organizational effectiveness – achieving human resource advantage by, as Boxall and Purcell (2003) point out, employing 'better people in organizations with better process' and generally creating 'a great place to work'.

3. Specific and articulated plans to create 'bundles' of HR practices and develop a coherent HR system. This can be achieved through the approaches summarized below.

4. The conscious introduction of overall approaches to human resource management such as high-performance management, high-involvement management and high-commitment management as described below. These overlap to a certain extent.

High-performance management

High-performance management aims to make an impact on the performance of the organization through its people in such areas as productivity, quality, levels of customer service, growth, profits and, ultimately, the delivery of increased shareholder value. High-performance management practices include rigorous recruitment and selection procedures, extensive and relevant training and management development activities, incentive pay systems and performance management processes. As a bundle, these practices are often called high-performance work systems (HPWS). This term is more frequently used than either high-involvement management or high-commitment management, although there is a degree of overlap between these approaches and an HPWS. High-performance work system strategies are considered in Chapter 9.

High-involvement management

The term 'high involvement' was used by Lawler (1986) to describe management systems based on commitment and involvement, as opposed to the old bureaucratic model based on control. The underlying hypothesis is that employees will increase their involvement with the company if they are given the opportunity to control and understand their work. He claimed that high-involvement practices worked well because they acted as a synergy and had a multiplicative effect. This approach involves treating employees as partners in the enterprise whose interests are respected and who have a voice on matters that concern them. It is concerned with communication and involvement. The aim is to create a climate in which a continuing dialogue between managers and the members of their teams takes place in order to define expectations and share information on the organization's mission, values and objectives. This establishes mutual understanding of what *is* to be achieved and a framework for managing and developing people to ensure that it *will* be achieved.

The practices included in a high-involvement system have sometimes expanded beyond this original concept and included high-performance practices. For example, as defined by Benson *et al* (2006), 'High-involvement work practices are a specific set of human resource practices that focus on employee decision-making, power, access to information, training and incentives.' As noted above, high-performance practices usually include relevant training and incentive pay systems. Sung and Ashton (2005) include high-involvement practices as one of the three broad areas of a high-performance work system (the other two being human resource practices and reward and commitment practices).

The way in which high involvement made an impact was explained by Guest (1997). He suggested that the commitment and flexibility provided by highly involving action lead to behaviour changes among employees. Because the employees show high levels of motivation, commitment and organizational citizenship, they adopt better-performing behaviours, leading to lower absenteeism and turnover rates, increased productivity and higher levels of quality.

High-commitment management

One of the defining characteristics of HRM is its emphasis on the importance of enhancing mutual commitment (Walton, 1985). High-commitment management has been described by Wood (1996) as 'A form of management which is aimed at eliciting a commitment so that behaviour is primarily self-regulated rather than controlled by sanctions and pressures external to the individual, and relations within the organization are based on high levels of trust.'

The approaches to achieving high commitment as described by Beer *et al* (1984) and Walton (1985) are:

▌ the development of career ladders and emphasis on trainability and commitment as highly valued characteristics of employees at all levels in the organization;

▌ a high level of functional flexibility, with the abandonment of potentially rigid job descriptions;

▌ the reduction of hierarchies and the ending of status differentials;

∎ a heavy reliance on team structure for disseminating information (team briefing), structuring work (teamworking) and problem solving (quality circles).

Wood and Albanese (1995) added to this list:

∎ job design as something management consciously does in order to provide jobs that have a considerable level of intrinsic satisfaction;
∎ a policy of no compulsory lay-offs or redundancies, and permanent employment guarantees, with the possible use of temporary workers to cushion fluctuations in the demand for labour;
∎ new forms of assessment and payment systems and, more specifically, merit pay and profit sharing;
∎ a high involvement of employees in the management of quality.

As defined above, high-involvement and high-commitment management have many similarities.

The following are some examples of overall HR strategy statements:

AEGON:

The Human Resources Integrated Approach aims to ensure that from whatever angle staff now look at the elements of pay management, performance, career development and reward, they are consistent and linked.

B&Q:

∎ Enhance employee commitment and minimize the loss of B&Q's best people.
∎ Position B&Q as one of the best employers in the UK.

Egg:

The major factor influencing HR strategy was the need to attract, maintain and retain the right people to deliver it. The aim was to introduce a system that complemented the business, that reflected the way we wanted to treat our customers – treating our people the same. What we would do for our customers we would also do for our people. We wanted to make an impact on the culture – the way people do business.

(HR director)

GlaxoSmithKline:

We want GSK to be a place where the best people do their best work.

An insurance company:

> Without the people in this business we don't have anything to deliver. We are driven to getting the people issues right in order to deliver the strategy. To a great extent it's the people that create and implement the strategy on behalf of the organization. We put people very much at the front of our strategic thought process. If we have the right people, the right training, the right qualifications and the right sort of culture then we can deliver our strategy. We cannot do it otherwise.

> (Chief executive)

Lands' End:

> Based on the principle that staff who are enjoying themselves, are being supported and developed, and who feel fulfilled and respected at work, will provide the best service to customers.

A local authority:

> [Our HR strategy is about] having a very strong focus on the overall effectiveness of the organization, its direction and how it's performing; here is commitment to, and belief in, and respect for individuals, and I think that these are very important factors.

> (Chief executive of a borough council)

A public utility:

> The only HR strategy you really need is the tangible expression of values and the implementation of values… unless you get the human resource values right you can forget all the rest.

> (Managing director)

A manufacturing company:

> The HR strategy is to stimulate changes on a broad front aimed ultimately at achieving competitive advantage through the efforts of our people. In an industry of fast followers, those who learn quickest will be the winners.

> (HR director)

A retail stores group:

> The biggest challenge will be to maintain [our] competitive advantage and to do that we need to maintain and continue to attract very high-calibre people. The key differentiator on anything any company does is fundamentally the people,

and I think that people tend to forget that they are the most important asset. Money is easy to get hold of; good people are not. All we do in terms of training and manpower planning is directly linked to business improvement.

(Managing director)

SPECIFIC HR STRATEGIES

Specific HR strategies set out what the organization intends to do in areas such as:

❚ *human capital management* – obtaining, analysing and reporting on data, which inform the direction of value-adding people management strategic, investment and operational decisions;

❚ *high-performance management* – developing and implementing high-performance work systems;

❚ *corporate social responsibility* – a commitment to managing the business ethically in order to make a positive impact on society and the environment;

❚ *organization development* – the planning and implementation of programmes designed to enhance the effectiveness with which an organization functions and responds to change;

❚ *engagement* – the development and implementation of policies designed to increase the level of employees' engagement with their work and the organization;

❚ *knowledge management* – creating, acquiring, capturing, sharing and using knowledge to enhance learning and performance;

❚ *resourcing* – attracting and retaining high-quality people;

❚ *talent management* – how the organization ensures that it has the talented people it needs to achieve success;

❚ *learning and development* – providing an environment in which employees are encouraged to learn and develop;

❚ *reward* – defining what the organization wants to do in the longer term to develop and implement reward policies, practices and processes that will further the achievement of its business goals and meet the needs of its stakeholders;

❚ *employee relations* – defining the intentions of the organization about what needs to be done and what needs to be changed in the ways in which the organization manages its relationships with employees and their trade unions.

The following are some examples of specific HR strategies:

The Children's Society:

- Implement the rewards strategy of the Society to support the corporate plan and secure the recruitment, retention and motivation of staff to deliver its business objectives.
- Manage the development of the human resources information system to secure productivity improvements in administrative processes.
- Introduce improved performance management processes for managers and staff of the Society.
- Implement training and development which supports the business objectives of the Society and improves the quality of work with children and young people.

Diageo:

There are three broad strands to the Organization and People Strategy:

1. *Reward and recognition:* use recognition and reward programmes to stimulate outstanding team and individual performance contributions.
2. *Talent management:* drive the attraction, retention and professional growth of a deep pool of diverse, talented employees.
3. *Organizational effectiveness:* ensure that the business adapts its organization to maximize employee contribution and deliver performance goals.

It provides direction to the company's talent, operational effectiveness and performance and reward agendas. The company's underlying thinking is that the people strategy is not for the human resource function to own but is the responsibility of the whole organization, hence the title 'Organization and People Strategy'.

A government agency:

The key components of the HR strategy are:

- Investing in people – improving the level of intellectual capital.
- Performance management – integrating the values contained in the HR strategy into performance management processes and ensuring that reviews concentrate on how well people are performing those values.
- Job design – a key component concerned with how jobs are designed and how they relate to the whole business.
- The reward system – in developing rewards strategies, taking into account that this is a very hard-driven business.

HR strategies for higher education institutions (the Higher Education Funding Council):

1. Address recruitment and retention difficulties in a targeted and cost-effective manner.

2. Meet specific staff development and training objectives that not only equip staff to meet their current needs but also prepare them for future changes, such as using new technologies for learning and teaching. This would include management development.

3. Develop equal opportunity targets with programmes to implement good practice throughout an institution. This would include ensuring equal pay for work of equal value, using institution-wide systems of job evaluation. This could involve institutions working collectively – regionally or nationally.

4. Carry out regular reviews of staffing needs, reflecting changes in market demands and technology. The reviews would consider overall numbers and the balance of different categories of staff.

5. Conduct annual performance reviews of all staff, based on open and objective criteria, with reward connected to the performance of individuals including, where appropriate, their contribution to teams.

6. Take action to tackle poor performance.

A local authority:

> The focus is on the organization of excellence. The strategy is broken down into eight sections: employee relations, recruitment and retention, training, performance management, pay and benefits, health and safety, absence management and equal opportunities.

CRITERIA FOR AN EFFECTIVE HR STRATEGY

An effective HR strategy is one that works in the sense that it achieves what it sets out to achieve. In particular, it:

- will satisfy business needs;
- will be founded on detailed analysis and study, not just wishful thinking;
- can be turned into actionable programmes that anticipate implementation requirements and problems;
- is coherent and integrated, being composed of components that fit with and support each other;
- takes account of the needs of line managers and employees generally as well as those of the organization and its other stakeholders. As Boxall and Purcell (2003) emphasize, 'HR planning should aim to meet the needs of the key stakeholder groups involved in people management in the firm.'

Here is a comment on what makes a good HR strategy:

> A good strategy is one which actually makes people feel valued. It makes them knowledgeable about the organization and makes them feel clear about where they sit as a group, or team, or individual. It must show them how what they do

either together or individually fits into that strategy. Importantly, it should indicate how people are going to be rewarded for their contribution and how they might be developed and grow in the organization.

(Chief executive, Peabody Trust)

HOW SHOULD HR STRATEGIES BE DEVELOPED?

When considering approaches to the formulation of HR strategy it is necessary to underline the interactive (not unilinear) relationship between business strategy and HRM, as have Hendry and Pettigrew (1990). They emphasize the limits of excessively rationalistic models of strategic and HR planning. The point that HR strategies are not necessarily developed formally and systematically but may instead evolve and emerge has been made by Tyson (1997): 'The process by which strategies come to be realized is not only through formal HR policies or written directions: strategy realization can also come from actions by managers and others. Since actions provoke reactions (acceptance, confrontation, negotiation etc) these reactions are also part of the strategy process.' Perhaps the best way to look at the reality of HR strategy formulation is to remember Mintzberg *et al*'s (1988) statement that strategy formulation is about 'preferences, choices, and matches' rather than an exercise 'in applied logic'. It is also desirable to follow Mintzberg's analysis and treat HR strategy as a perspective rather than a rigorous procedure for mapping the future. Moore (1992) has suggested that Mintzberg has looked inside the organization, indeed inside the heads of the collective strategists, and come to the conclusion that, relative to the organization, strategy is analogous to the personality of an individual. As Mintzberg sees them, all strategies exist in the minds of those people they make an impact upon. What is important is that people in the organization share the same perspective 'through their intentions and/or by their actions'. This is what Mintzberg calls the collective mind, and reading that mind is essential if we are 'to understand how intentions... become shared, and how action comes to be exercised on a collective yet consistent basis'.

Propositions on formulating HR strategy

Boxall (1993) has drawn up the following propositions about the formulation of HR strategy from the literature:

▌ The strategy formation process is complex, and excessively rationalistic models that advocate formalistic linkages between strategic planning and HR planning are not particularly helpful to our understanding of it.

▌ Business strategy may be an important influence on HR strategy but it is only one of several factors.

▌ Implicit (if not explicit) in the mix of factors that influence the shape of HR strategies is a set of historical compromises and trade-offs from stakeholders.

It is also necessary to stress that coherent and integrated HR strategies are only likely to be developed if the top team understands and acts upon the strategic imperatives associated with the employment, development and engagement of people. This will be achieved more effectively if there is an HR director who is playing an active and respected role as a member of the top management team. A further consideration is that the effective implementation of HR strategies depends on the involvement, commitment and cooperation of line managers and staff generally. Finally, there is too often a wide gap between the rhetoric of strategic HRM and the reality of its impact, as Gratton *et al* (1999) emphasize. Good intentions can too easily be subverted by the harsh realities of organizational life. For example, strategic objectives such as increasing commitment by providing more security and offering training to increase employability may have to be abandoned or at least modified because of the short-term demands made on the business to increase shareholder value.

Schools of strategy development

Purcell (2001) has identified three main schools of strategy development: the design school, the process school and the configuration school.

The design school is deliberate and is 'based on the assumption of economic rationality'. It uses quantitative rather than qualitative tools of analysis and focuses on market opportunities and threats. What happens inside the company is 'mere administration or operations'.

The process school adopts a variety of approaches and is concerned with how strategies are made and what influences strategy formulation: 'It is much more a study of what actually happens with explanations coming from experience rather than deductive theory.' As Purcell suggests, the implication of the design concept is that 'everything is possible' while that of the process school is that 'little can be done except swim with the tide of events'. The rationalist approach adopted by Purcell's design school broadly corresponds with the classical approach to strategy, and Porter is a typical representative of it. Purcell's process school is the postmodern version of strategy of which Mintzberg is the most notable exponent. But, as Grant (1991) has indicated, the rationalist approach may indeed be over-formalized and rely too much on quantitative data, but the Mintzberg approach, which downplays the role of systematic analysis and emphasizes the role of intuition and vision, fails to provide a clear basis for reasoned choices.

The configuration school draws attention to the beliefs that, first, strategies vary according to the life cycle of the organization, second, they will be contingent on the sector of the organization and, third, they will be about change and transformation. The focus is on implementation strategies, which is where Purcell thinks HR can play a major role.

Levels of strategic decision making

Ideally, the formulation of HR strategies is conceived as a process that is closely aligned to the formulation of business strategies. HR strategy can influence as well as be influenced by business strategy.

Research conducted by Wright *et al* (2004) identified two approaches that can be adopted by HR to strategy formulation: the inside-out approach and the outside-in approach. They made the following observations about the HR–strategy linkage:

> At the extreme, the 'inside-out' approach begins with the status quo HR function (in terms of skills, processes, technologies etc) and then attempts (with varying degrees of success) to identify linkages to the business (usually through focusing on 'people issues'), making minor adjustments to HR activities along the way... On the other hand, a few firms have made a paradynamic shift to build their HR strategies from the starting point of the business. Within these 'outside-in' HR functions, the starting point is the business, including the customer, competitor and business issues they face. The HR strategy then derives directly from these challenges to create real solutions and add real value.

They made the point that 'the most advanced linkage was the "integrative" linkage in which the senior HR executive was part of the top management team, and was able to sit at the table and contribute during development of the business strategy'.

In reality, however, HR strategies are more likely to flow from business strategies, which will be dominated by product/market and financial considerations. But there is still room for HR to make a useful, even essential, contribution at the stage when business strategies are conceived, for example by focusing on resource issues. This contribution may be more significant if strategy formulation is an emergent or evolutionary process – HR strategic issues will then be dealt with as they arise during the course of formulating and implementing the corporate strategy.

A distinction is made by Purcell (1989) and Purcell and Ahlstrand (1994) between:

▌ *'upstream' first-order decisions*, which are concerned with the long-term direction of the enterprise or the scope of its activities;

▌ *'downstream' second-order decisions*, which are concerned with internal operating procedures and how the firm is organized to achieve its goals; and

▌ *'downstream' third-order decisions*, which are concerned with choices on human resource structures and approaches and are strategic in the sense that they establish the basic parameters of employee relations management in the firm.

It can indeed be argued that HR strategies, like other functional strategies such as product development, manufacturing and the introduction of new technology, will be developed within the context of the overall business strategy, but this need not imply that HR strategies come third in the pecking order.

Strategic options and choices

The process of developing HR strategies involves generating strategic HRM options and then making appropriate strategic choices. It has been noted by Cappelli (1999) that 'The choice of practices that an employer pursues is heavily contingent on a number of factors at the organizational level, including their own business and production strategies, support of HR policies, and cooperative labour relations.' The process of developing HR strategies involves the adoption of a contingent approach in generating strategic HRM options and then making appropriate strategic choices. There is seldom if ever one right way forward.

Choices should relate to but also anticipate the critical needs of the business. They should be founded on detailed analysis and study, not just wishful thinking, and should incorporate the experienced and collective judgement of top management about the organizational requirements while also taking into account the needs of line managers and employees generally. The emerging strategies should anticipate the problems of implementation that may arise if line managers are not committed to the strategy and/or lack the skills and time to play their part, and the strategies should be capable of being turned into actionable programmes. Consideration needs to be given to the impact of the five forces on HR policy choice identified by Baron and Kreps (1999):

1. the external environment (social, political, legal and economic);
2. the workforce;
3. the organization's culture;
4. the organization's strategy;
5. the technology of production and organization of work.

DEVELOPING HR STRATEGIES

Five fundamental questions that need to be asked in formulating HR strategies have been posed by Becker and Huselid (1998):

1. What are the firm's strategic objectives?
2. How are these translated into unit objectives?
3. What do unit managers consider are the 'performance drivers' of those objectives?
4. How do the skills, motivation and structure of the firm's workforce influence these performance drivers?
5. How does the HR system influence the skills, motivation and structure of the workforce?

The following six-step approach is proposed by Gratton (2000):

1. *Build the guiding coalition* – involve people from all parts of the business.
2. *Image the future* – create a shared vision of areas of strategic importance.
3. *Understand current capabilities and identify the gap* – establish 'where the organization is now and the gap between aspirations for the future and the reality of the present'.
4. *Create a map of the system* – 'ensure that the parts can be built into a meaningful whole'.
5. *Model the dynamics of the system* – ensure that the dynamic nature of the future is taken into account.
6. *Bridge into action* – agree the broad themes for action and the specific issues related to those themes, develop guiding principles, involve line managers and create cross-functional teams to identify goals and performance indicators.

But many different routes may be followed when formulating HR strategies – there is no one right way. On the basis of their research in 30 well-known companies, Tyson and Witcher (1994) commented that 'The different approaches to strategy formation reflect different ways to manage change and different ways to bring the people part of the business into line with business goals.'

In developing HR strategies, process may be as important as content. Tyson and Witcher (1994) also noted from their research that 'The process of formulating HR strategy was often as important as the content of the strategy ultimately agreed. It was argued that by working through strategic issues and highlighting points of tension, new ideas emerged and a consensus over goals was found.'

A methodology for formulating HR strategies

A methodology for formulating HR strategies was developed by Dyer and Holder (1988) as follows:

1. *Assess feasibility.* From an HR point of view, feasibility depends on whether the numbers and types of key people required to make the proposal succeed can be obtained on a timely basis and at a reasonable cost, and whether the behavioural expectations assumed by the strategy are realistic (eg retention rates and productivity levels).
2. *Determine desirability.* Examine the implications of strategy in terms of sacrosanct HR policies (eg a strategy of rapid retrenchment would have to be called into question by a company with a full employment policy).
3. *Determine goals.* These indicate the main issues to be worked on and they derive primarily from the content of the business strategy. For example, a strategy to become a lower-cost producer would require the reduction of labour costs. This in turn translates into two types of HR goals: higher performance standards (contribution) and reduced head-counts (composition).
4. *Decide means of achieving goals.* The general rule is that the closer the external and internal fit, the better the strategy, consistent with the need to adapt flexibly to change. External fit refers to the degree of consistency between HR goals on the one hand and the exigencies of the underlying business strategy and relevant environmental conditions on the other. Internal fit measures the extent to which HR means follow from the HR goals and other relevant environmental conditions, as well as the degree of coherency or synergy among the various HR means.

Achieving vertical fit – integrating business and HR strategies

Wright and Snell (1998) suggest that seeking fit requires knowledge of the skills and behaviour necessary to implement the strategy, knowledge of the HRM practices necessary to elicit those skills and behaviours and the ability to quickly implement the desired system of HRM practices.

When considering how to integrate business and HR strategies it should be remembered that business and HR issues influence each other and in turn influence corporate and business unit strategies. It is also necessary to note that, in establishing these links, account must be taken of the fact that strategies for change have also to be integrated with changes in the external and internal environments. Fit may exist at a point in time, but circumstances will change and fit no longer exists. An excessive pursuit of 'fit' with the status quo will inhibit the flexibility of approach that is essential in turbulent conditions. This is the 'temporal' factor in achieving fit identified by Gratton *et al* (1999). An additional factor that will make the achievement of good vertical fit difficult is that the business strategy may not be clearly defined – it could be in an emergent or evolutionary state. This would mean that there could be nothing with which to fit the HR strategy.

Achieving horizontal integration (bundling)

Horizontal integration or fit is achieved when the various HR strategies cohere and are mutually supporting. This can be attained by the process of 'bundling' as described in Chapter 3. Bundling is carried out by first identifying appropriate HR practices, second, assessing how the items in the bundle can be linked together so that they become mutually reinforcing and therefore coherent, which may mean identifying integrating processes, and finally drawing up programmes for the development of these practices, paying particular attention to the links between them.

Integrative processes

The use of high-performance, high-involvement or high-commitment systems as described earlier in this chapter is an integrating process. The essence of these systems is that they each consist of a set of complementary work practices that are developed and maintained as a whole. Another integrating activity is talent management as described in Chapter 15.

Within these systems or as distinct approaches, two frequently used integrating processes are performance management and the use of competencies. The ways in which they link different HR practices are illustrated in Figures 4.1 and 4.2.

Horizontal integration can also be achieved by the development of career family grading structures, which define the competencies required at each level, thus indicating career paths, and also serve as the framework for pay structures.

Setting out the strategy

There is no standard model of how an HR strategy should be set out. It all depends on the circumstances of the organization. But the following are the typical areas that may be covered in a written strategy:

1. *Basis:*
   - business needs in terms of the key elements of the business strategy;
   - environmental factors and analysis (SWOT / PESTLE);
   - cultural factors: possible helps or hindrances to implementation.
2. *Content: details of the proposed HR strategy.*
3. *Rationale:* the business case for the strategy against the background of business needs and environmental / cultural factors.

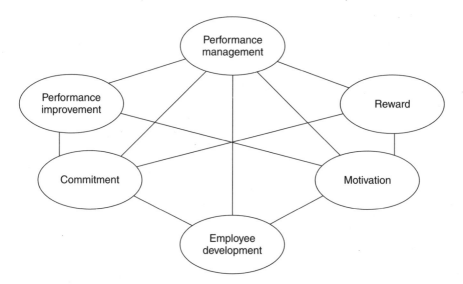

Figure 4.1 Performance management as an integrating force

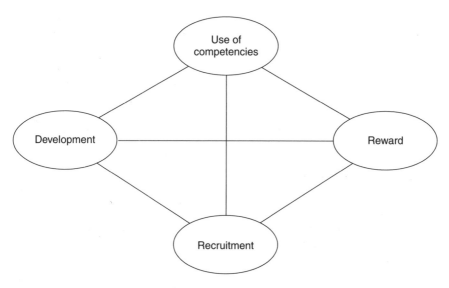

Figure 4.2 Use of competencies as an integrating force

4. *Implementation plan:*
   - action programme;
   - responsibility for each stage;
   - resources required;
   - proposed arrangements for communication, consultation, involvement and training;
   - project management arrangements.

5. *Costs and benefits analysis:* an assessment of the resource implications of the plan (costs, people and facilities) and the benefits that will accrue, for the organization as a whole, for line managers and for individual employees (so far as possible these benefits should be quantified in terms of return on investment or value added).

IMPLEMENTING HR STRATEGIES

Because strategies tend to be expressed as abstractions, they must be translated into programmes with clearly stated objectives and deliverables. It is necessary to avoid saying, in effect, 'We need to get from here to there but we don't care how.' But getting strategies into action is not easy. Too often, strategists act like Mr Pecksmith, who was compared by Dickens (1843) to 'a direction-post which is always telling the way to a place and never goes there'.

The term 'strategic HRM' has been devalued in some quarters, sometimes to mean no more than a few generalized ideas about HR policies and at other times to describe a short-term plan, for example to increase the retention rate of graduates. It must be emphasized that HR strategies are not just programmes, policies or plans concerning HR issues that the HR department happens to feel are important. Piecemeal initiatives do not constitute strategy.

The problem with strategic HRM as noted by Gratton *et al* (1999) is that too often there is a gap between what the strategy states will be achieved and what actually happens to it. As they put it:

> One principal strand that has run through this entire book is the disjunction between rhetoric and reality in the area of human resource management, between HRM theory and HRM practice, between what the HR function says it is doing and how that practice is perceived by employees, and between what senior management believes to be the role of the HR function, and the role it actually plays.

The factors identified by Gratton *et al* that contribute to creating this gap included:

▮ the tendency of employees in diverse organizations only to accept initiatives they perceive to be relevant to their own areas;
▮ the tendency of long-serving employees to cling to the status quo;
▮ complex or ambiguous initiatives may not be understood by employees or will be perceived differently by them, especially in large, diverse organizations;

▌ it is more difficult to gain acceptance of non-routine initiatives;

▌ employees will be hostile to initiatives if the initiatives are believed to be in conflict with the organization's identity, eg downsizing in a culture of 'job-for-life';

▌ the initiative is seen as a threat;

▌ inconsistencies between corporate strategies and values;

▌ the extent to which senior management is trusted;

▌ the perceived fairness of the initiative;

▌ the extent to which existing processes could help to embed the initiative;

▌ a bureaucratic culture that leads to inertia.

Barriers to the implementation of HR strategies

Each of the factors listed by Gratton *et al* can create barriers to the successful implementation of HR strategies. Other major barriers include failure to understand the strategic needs of the business, inadequate assessment of the environmental and cultural factors that affect the content of the strategies, and the development of ill-conceived and irrelevant initiatives, possibly because they are current fads or because there has been an ill-digested analysis of best practice that does not fit the organization's requirements. These problems are compounded when insufficient attention is paid to practical implementation problems, the important role of line managers in implementing strategies and the need to have established supporting processes for the initiative (eg performance management to support performance pay).

Overcoming the barriers

To overcome these barriers it is necessary to: 1) conduct a rigorous preliminary analysis of needs and requirements; 2) formulate the strategy; 3) enlist support for the strategy; 4) assess barriers; 5) prepare action plans; 6) project-manage implementation; and 7) follow up and evaluate progress so that remedial action can be taken as necessary.

5

The strategic role of HR

It has been emphasized a number of times so far in this book that strategic HRM is not just about strategic planning. It is equally, if not more, concerned with the implementation of strategy and the strategic behaviour of HR specialists working with their line management colleagues on an everyday basis to ensure that the business goals of the organization are achieved and its values are put into practice. The strategic role of HR professionals is examined in this chapter, which starts with an overview of the strategic nature of HR and continues with discussions of the business partner model and what 'being strategic' means. The chapter concludes with analyses of the roles of HR directors, HR business partners and HR advisers or assistants.

THE STRATEGIC NATURE OF HR

The work of HR practitioners can be divided into two main areas: transactional activities and strategic activities. Transactional activities consist of the service delivery aspects of HR – recruitment, training, dealing with people issues, legal compliance and employee services. HR strategic activities support the achievement of the organization's goals and values and involve the development and implementation of forward-looking HR strategies that are integrated with one another and aligned to business objectives. Importantly, HR strategic activities also involve HR practitioners working with their line management colleagues in the continuous development and implementation of the business strategy. HR has to get its service delivery activities right – that's what it's there to do, day by day, and its reputation with line managers largely depends on this. But in accordance with the resource-based view, which emphasizes the importance of human capital in achieving competitive advantage, the credibility of HR also depends on its ability to make a strategic contribution that ensures that the organization has the quality of skilled, motivated and engaged people it needs. The strategic nature of HR has been expressed in the strategic partner model as described below.

THE STRATEGIC PARTNER MODEL

HR practitioners share responsibility with their line management colleagues for the success of the enterprise. In 1985, Tyson, anticipating Ulrich by 13 years, described them as business managers who have the capacity to identify business opportunities, to see the broad picture and to understand how their role can help to achieve the company's business objectives. They integrate their activities closely with top management and ensure that they serve a long-term strategic purpose. They anticipate needs, act flexibly and are proactive.

The David Ulrich model

David Ulrich (1998) argued that HR professionals carry out the following proactive roles as champions of competitiveness in creating and delivering value:

1. *strategic partners* helping the business to successfully implement strategy;
2. *administrative experts* improving organizational efficiency by re-engineering the HR function and other work processes;
3. *employee champions* maximizing employee commitment and competence and their overall responsiveness to change;
4. *change agents* delivering organizational transformation and culture change.

This model was reformulated by Ulrich and Brockbank in 2005 to list the following roles:

▮ *Strategic partner* – consists of multiple dimensions: business expert, change agent, strategic HR planner, knowledge manager and consultant; combining them to align HR systems to help accomplish the organization's vision and mission, helping managers to get things done, and disseminating learning across the organization.

▌ *Employee advocate* – focuses on the needs of today's employees through listening, understanding and empathizing.

▌ *Human capital developer* – in the role of managing and developing human capital (individuals and teams), focuses on preparing employees to be successful in the future.

▌ *Functional expert* – concerned with the HR practices that are central to HR value, acting with insight on the basis of the body of knowledge possessed. Some are delivered through administrative efficiency (such as technology or process design), and others through policies, menus and interventions. Necessary to distinguish between the foundation HR practices – recruitment, learning and development, rewards, etc – and the emerging HR practices such as communications, work process and organization design, and executive leadership development.

▌ *Leader* – leading the HR function, collaborating with other functions and providing leadership to them, setting and enhancing the standards for strategic thinking and ensuring corporate governance.

Business partnering

The concept of business partnering has been enthusiastically adopted by the Chartered Institute of Personnel and Development (2007a). The term 'business partner' was defined loosely as covering 'a diversity of jobs from strategic to administrative to consultancy'. According to the CIPD, business partnering 'makes HR accountable to the business, and expects HR to add real value'. It involves the restructuring of HR into three specialist functions: shared services, centres of excellence and strategic partners. The latter consists of a few HR professionals working closely with business leaders, influencing strategy and steering its implementation. The task of strategic partners is to ensure the business makes the best use of its people and its people opportunities. The role is to highlight the HR issues and possibilities that executives don't often see. It also aims to inform and shape HR strategy, so that, as business partners, HR practitioners work closely with their line management colleagues. They are aware of business strategies and the opportunities and threats facing the organization. They are capable of analysing organizational strengths and weaknesses and diagnosing the issues facing the enterprise and their human resource implications. They know about the critical success factors that will create competitive advantage, and they can draw up a convincing business case for innovations that will add value.

The term 'added value' looms large in the concept of the HR business partner. It is often used rhetorically. In accounting language, where the phrase originated, added value is defined as the value added to the cost of raw materials and bought-out parts by the process of production and distribution. In HR speak, added value seems to mean the contribution made by

HR to business success, which is measured by the extent to which the value of that contribution exceeds its cost. Francis and Keegan (2006) report this comment from a recruitment consultant, which illustrates how the term has become popular: 'Most HR professionals will now have "value added" stamped on their foreheads, because they are always being asked to think in terms of the business objectives and how what they do supports the business objectives and the business plan.'

However, it can be argued that too much has been made of the business partner model. Perhaps it is preferable to emphasize that the role of HR professionals is to be *part* of the business rather than merely being partners. Tim Miller, group HR director of Standard Chartered Bank, as reported by Smethurst (2005), dislikes the term: 'Give me a break!' he says. 'It's so demeaning. How many people in marketing or finance have to say they are a partner in the business? Why do we have to think that we're not an intimate part of the business, just like sales, manufacturing and engineering? I detest and loathe the term and I won't use it.' Another leading group HR director, Alex Wilson of BT, as reported by Pickard (2005), is equally hostile. He says:

> The term worries me to death. HR has to be an integral and fundamental part of developing the strategy of the business. I don't even like the term close to the business because, like business partner it implies we are working alongside our line management colleagues but on a separate track, rather than people management being an integral part of the business.

WHAT BEING STRATEGIC MEANS

The term 'business partner' may not be generally accepted but there is a universal chorus of approval for the notion that HR professionals need to be strategic. However, what 'being strategic' means is not always made clear. It sounds good but what do HR people actually do when they are acting strategically? And is the process of being strategic reserved for those at the top or is it something that everyone in HR does?

An answer to the first question is provided by the CIPD in its Professional Standards (2004), where one of the competencies is strategic capability, defined as 'The capacity to create an achievable vision for the future, to foresee longer-term developments, to envisage options (and their probable consequences), to select sound courses of action, to rise above the day-to-day detail, to challenge the status quo.'

The problem with this definition is that it seems to dwell on what HR directors and heads of HR functions in centres of expertise do rather than provide a realistic picture of the roles of more junior HR specialists. The latter may aspire to be strategic later in their careers and they will do their jobs better if they understand how they contribute to attaining the organization's goals, but someone in a service centre administering a recruitment exercise or advising on how to handle a disciplinary problem will not be spending much time on creating an 'achievable vision for the future' let alone foreseeing longer-term developments or challenging the status quo. The research conducted by Francis and Keegan (2006) elicited the following comment from a CIPD course tutor about student practitioners: 'It is complicated by the fact that the majority of their concerns are operational rather than strategic and there seems to be an increasing divergence between their needs/concerns and the content of the CIPD programme.' A student remarked to the researchers that the CIPD thought that they would all be strategic business partners 'and we're not you know, we have to deal with day-to-day HR issues that arise in the business'.

The CIPD (2005) has supported the focus on strategic capability with the concept of the 'thinking performer', to the effect that: 'All personnel and development specialists must be thinking performers. That is, their central task is to be knowledgeable and competent in their various fields and to be able to move beyond compliance to provide a critique of organizational policies and procedures and to advise on how organizations should develop in the future.'

This concept can be interpreted as meaning that HR professionals have to think carefully about what they are doing in the context of their organization and within the framework of a recognized body of knowledge, and they have to perform effectively in the sense of delivering advice, guidance and services that will help the organization to achieve its strategic goals. But the extent to which more junior practitioners 'advise on how organizations should develop in the future' may well be limited.

A more realistic assessment of what being strategic means can be produced by analysing what is involved at different levels: HR directors, heads of major HR functions (learning and development, reward, etc) who may be in centres of expertise, business partners embedded in operational departments, and HR advisers or assistants who may be working in shared service centres.

THE STRATEGIC ROLE OF HR DIRECTORS

The strategic role of HR directors is to promote the achievement of the organization's business goals by 1) developing and implementing HR strategies that are integrated with the business strategy and are coherent and mutually supportive and 2) ensuring that a strategic approach is adopted by the HR function that supports the business and adds value. To carry out this role the HR director should:

- understand the strategic goals of the organization;
- appreciate the business imperatives and performance drivers relative to these goals;
- comprehend how sustainable competitive advantage can be obtained through the human capital of the organization and know how HR practices can contribute to the achievement of strategic goals;
- contribute to the development of the business strategy on an 'outside-in' basis as described in Chapter 4 by emphasizing how the organization's distinctive human resources can make an impact;
- contribute to the development for the business of a clear vision and a set of integrated values;
- ensure that senior management understands the HR implications of its business strategy;
- be aware of the broader context (the competitive environment and the business, economic, social and legal factors that affect it) in which the organization operates;
- understand the kinds of employee behaviour required successfully to execute the business strategy;
- think in terms of the bigger and longer-term picture of where HR should go and how to get there;
- believe in and practise evidence-based management;
- be capable of making a powerful business case for any proposals on the development of HR strategies.

THE STRATEGIC ROLE OF HEADS OF HR FUNCTIONS

The strategic role of heads of HR functions is fundamentally the same for their function as that of HR directors for the whole organization. They promote the achievement of the organization's business goals by developing and implementing functional strategies that are aligned with the business strategy and integrated with the strategies for other HR functions and adopt a strategic approach in the sense of ensuring that HR activities support the business and add value. To carry out this role heads of HR functions should:

- understand the strategic goals of the organization as they affect their function;
- appreciate the business imperatives and performance drivers relative to these goals;
- help senior management to understand the implications of its strategy for the HR function;
- know how HR practices in the function can contribute to the achievement of the strategic goals;

∎ ensure that their activities provide added value for the organization;
∎ be aware of the broader context (the competitive environment and the business, economic, social and legal factors that affect it) in which the function operates;
∎ think in terms of the bigger and longer-term picture of where HR strategies for the function should go and how to get there;
∎ believe in and practise evidence-based management;
∎ be capable of making a powerful business case for any proposals on the development of HR strategies for the function.

THE STRATEGIC ROLE OF HR BUSINESS PARTNERS

The strategic role of HR business partners is to promote the achievement of the business goals of the organizational unit or function in which they operate. To carry out this role they should:

∎ understand the business and its competitive environment;
∎ understand the goals of their part of the business and its plans to attain them;
∎ ensure that their activities provide added value for the unit or function;
∎ build relationships founded on trust with their line management clients;
∎ provide support to the strategic activities of their colleagues;
∎ align their activities with business requirements;
∎ believe in and practise evidence-based management;
∎ be proactive, anticipating requirements, identifying problems and producing innovative and evidence-based solutions to them;
∎ see the broad picture and rise above the day-to-day detail.

THE STRATEGIC CONTRIBUTION OF HR ADVISERS OR ASSISTANTS

The role of HR advisers or assistants is primarily that of delivering effective HR services within their function or as members of an HR service centre. While they will not be responsible for the formulation of HR strategies they may contribute to them within their own speciality. They will need to understand the business goals of the departments or managers for whom they provide services in order to ensure that these services support the achievement of those goals.

6

The impact of strategic HRM

Strategic HRM aims to improve business performance through people and to meet the needs of the organization's employees. Employee well-being is or should be a major concern, but organizations in all sectors (private, public or voluntary) have to be businesslike in the sense that they are in the business of effectively and efficiently achieving their purpose whether this is to make profits, deliver a public service or undertake charitable functions. A considerable amount of research has been conducted recently on how HRM impacts on organizational performance, and this is summarized in the next section of this chapter. The chapter then explores the general lessons that can be learnt from this research and other relevant research projects. Finally, consideration is given to how, in the light of the research, strategic HRM can make a contribution to improving business performance.

HOW HR IMPACTS ON ORGANIZATIONAL PERFORMANCE

The assumption underpinning the practice of HRM is that people are the organization's key resource and organizational performance largely depends on them. If, therefore, an appropriate range of HR policies and processes is developed and implemented effectively, then HR will make a substantial impact on firm performance.

The holy grail sought by many commentators on human resource management is to establish that a clear positive link between HRM practices and organizational performance exists. There has been much research, as summarized in Table 6.1, over the last decade or so that has attempted to answer two basic questions: 'Do HR practices make a positive impact on organizational performance?'; 'If so, how is the impact achieved?' The second question is the more important one. It is not enough to justify HRM by proving that it is a good thing. What counts is what can be done to ensure that it *is* a good thing. This is the 'black box' mentioned by Purcell *et al* (2003) that lies between intentions and outcomes.

Ulrich (1997) has pointed out that: 'HR practices seem to matter; logic says it is so; survey findings confirm it. Direct relationships between investment and attention to HR practices are often fuzzy, however, and vary according to the population sampled and the measures used.'

Purcell *et al* (2003) have cast doubts on the validity of some of the attempts through research to make the connection: 'Our study has demonstrated convincingly that research which only asks about the number and extent of

Table 6.1   Research on the link between HRM and firm performance

Researcher(s)	Methodology	Outcomes
Arthur (1990, 1992, 1994)	Data from 30 US strip mills used to assess impact on labour efficiency and scrap rate by reference to the existence of either a high-commitment strategy or a control strategy.	Firms with a high-commitment strategy had significantly higher levels of both productivity and quality than those with a control strategy.
Huselid (1995)	Analysis of the responses of 968 US firms to a questionnaire exploring the use of high-performance work practices, the development of synergies between them and the alignment of these practices with the competitive strategy.	Productivity is influenced by employee motivation; financial performance is influenced by employee skills, motivation and organizational structures.
Huselid and Becker (1996)	An index of HR systems in 740 firms was created to indicate the degree to which each firm adopted a high-performance work system.	Firms with high values on the index had economically and statistically higher levels of performance.
Becker et al (1997)	Outcomes of a number of research projects were analysed to assess the strategic impact on shareholder value of high-performance work systems.	High-performance systems make an impact as long as they are embedded in the management infrastructure.

Researcher(s)	Methodology	Outcomes
Patterson et al (1997)	The research examined the link between business performance and organization culture and the use of a number of HR practices.	HR practices explained significant variations in profitability and productivity (19 per cent and 1 per cent respectively). Two HR practices were particularly significant: 1) the acquisition and development of employee skills; and 2) job design, including flexibility, responsibility, variety and the use of formal teams.
The 1998 Workplace Employee Relations Survey (as analysed by Guest et al, 2000a)	An analysis of the survey, which sampled some 2,000 workplaces and obtained the views of about 28,000 employees.	A strong association exists between HRM and both employee attitudes and workplace performance.
The Future of Work Survey, Guest et al (2000b)	835 private sector organizations were surveyed and interviews were carried out with 610 HR professionals and 462 chief executives.	A greater use of HR practices is associated with higher levels of employee commitment and contribution and is in turn linked to higher levels of productivity and quality of services.
Thompson (2002)	A study of the impact of high-performance work practices such as teamworking, appraisal, job rotation, broad-banded grade structures and sharing of business information in 623 UK aerospace establishments.	The number of HR practices and the proportion of the workforce covered appeared to be the key differentiating factor between more and less successful firms.
West et al (2002)	Research conducted in 61 UK hospitals obtaining information on HR strategy, policy and procedures from chief executives and HR directors, and mortality rates.	An association between certain HR practices and lower mortality rates was identified. As noted by Professor West: 'If you have HR practices that focus on effort and skill; develop people's skills; encourage co-operation, collaboration, innovation and synergy in teams for most, if not all employees, the whole system functions and performs better.'
Guest et al (2003)	An exploration of the relationship between HRM and performance in 366 UK companies using objective and subjective performance data and cross-sectional and longitudinal data.	Some evidence was shown of an association between HRM, as described by the number of HR practices in use, and performance, but there was no convincing indication that the greater application of HRM is likely to result in improved corporate performance.

Table 6.1   continued

Researcher(s)	Methodology	Outcomes
Purcell *et al* (2003)	A University of Bath longitudinal study of 12 companies to establish how people management impacts on organizational performance.	The most successful companies had what the researchers called 'the big idea'. The companies had a clear vision and a set of integrated values that were embedded, enduring, collective, measured and managed. They were concerned with sustaining performance and flexibility. Clear evidence existed between positive attitudes towards HR policies and practices, levels of satisfaction, motivation and commitment, and operational performance. Policy and practice implementation (not the number of HR practices adopted) is the vital ingredient in linking people management to business performance, and this is primarily the task of line managers.

HR practices can never be sufficient to understand the link between HR practices and business performance. As we have discussed it is misleading to assume that simply because HR policies are present that they will be implemented as intended.'

How HRM strategies make an impact

In Guest *et al* (2000b) the relationship between HRM and performance was modelled as shown in Figure 6.1.

The Bath people and performance model developed by Purcell *et al* (2003) is shown in Figure 6.2.

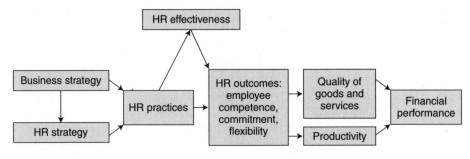

Figure 6.1   Model of a link between HRM and performance

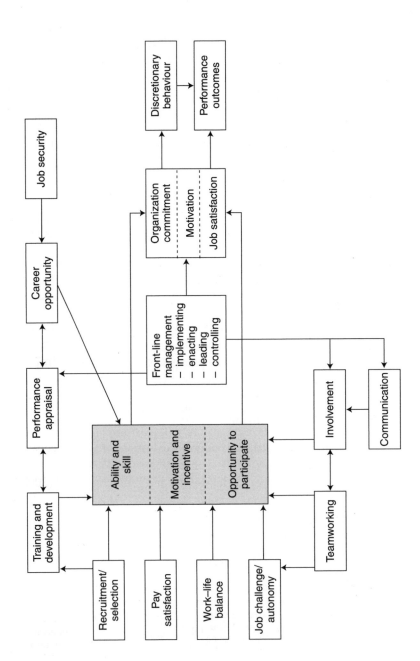

Figure 6.2 The Bath people and performance model

Table 6.2 The HR practices that impact on performance

HR Practice Area	How It Impacts
Attracting, developing and retaining high-quality people	Matches people to the strategic and operational needs of the organization. Provides for the acquisition, development and retention of talented employees, who can deliver superior performance, productivity, flexibility, innovation, and high levels of personal customer service and who 'fit' the culture and the strategic requirements of the organization.
Talent management	Ensures that the talented and well-motivated people required by the organization to meet present and future needs are available.
Working environment – core values, leadership, work–life balance, managing diversity, secure employment	Develops 'the big idea' (Purcell et al, 2003), ie a clear vision and a set of integrated values. Makes the organization 'a great place to work'.
Job and work design	Provides individuals with stimulating and interesting work and gives them the autonomy and flexibility to perform these jobs well. Enhances job satisfaction and flexibility, which encourages greater performance and productivity.
Learning and development	Enlarges the skill base and develops the levels of competence required in the workforce. Encourages discretionary learning, which happens when individuals actively seek to acquire the knowledge and skills that promote the organization's objectives. Develops a climate of learning – a growth medium in which self-managed learning as well as coaching, mentoring and training flourish.
Managing knowledge and intellectual capital	Focuses on both organizational and individual learning and provides learning opportunities and opportunities to share knowledge in a systematic way. Ensures vital stocks of knowledge are retained and improves the flow of knowledge, information and learning within the organization.
Increasing engagement, commitment and motivation	Encourages people to identify themselves with and act upon the core values of the organization and willingly to contribute to the achievement of organizational goals. Develops a climate of cooperation and trust; clarifies the psychological contract.
High-performance management	Develops a performance culture that encourages high performance in such areas as productivity, quality, levels of customer service, growth, profits and, ultimately, the delivery of increased shareholder value. Empowers employees to exhibit the discretionary behaviours most closely associated with higher business performance, such as risk taking, innovation and sharing of knowledge, and establishes trust between managers and subordinates.
Reward management	Develops motivation, commitment and job engagement by valuing them in accordance with their contribution.

Central to this model is the concept that performance is a function of Ability + Motivation + Opportunity (AMO). On the outside ring 11 policy or practice areas are identified to feed into and give meaning to AMO. The second crucial feature of the model is the central box – front-line management – which draws attention to the fact that nearly all HR policies are applied through and by line managers. It is these managers who bring policies to life. Organizational commitment, motivation and job satisfaction all lead to discretionary behaviour, which in turn generates performance outcomes, which in themselves contribute to commitment, motivation and job satisfaction.

HOW STRATEGIC HRM CONCEPTS IMPACT ON PRACTICE

The practice areas covered by HR strategies that impact on performance are summarized in Table 6.2.

7

Strategic HRM in action

This chapter contains illustrations of strategic HRM in action under the following headings:

▌ formulating HR strategy;
▌ the content of HR strategies;
▌ corporate issues;
▌ achieving integration;
▌ summary of the most characteristic features of strategic HRM in action.

FORMULATING HR STRATEGY

Taking into account Tyson and Witcher's (1994) point that you can only study HR strategy in the context of business strategies, the processes of formulating both business and HR strategies in a number of organizations are described below.

ABC Distribution

ABC Distribution distributes food products, mainly to major retailers. The critical success factors for the organization as spelt out by its managing director and the finance director are its ability to meet its profit targets and to grow the business substantially on a consistent basis by developing a reputation for providing added-value services, developing business with existing customers, winning new customers, and acquisitions. The company has doubled in size in the last four years. Underpinning the development of the company are the needs to grow the infrastructure, to develop management and leadership and to extend quality and safety programmes.

Business strategy

The managing director agreed that in a sense their business strategy evolved in a semi-formal way, but this evolution took place 'by the key people understanding what the total business was trying to do, and their part in it; then they went away and put their bits together; then we pulled all of it together'. He commented that 'Our strategy is very simple and very broad. It can be put down in a few sentences. It's what lies around it that has to be developed.' He emphasized that 'We sought to demonstrate to the rest of the business that we [the board] were a team. Where a team hadn't existed before, a team was now running the company.'

The deputy managing director explained how he saw the formulation of the business strategy taking place: 'We put our strategy together within the framework of the financial targets we have to meet and our values for quality, integrity and management style.' In answer to the question 'How does your organization develop its business strategies?' the director of finance said:

> It started off as being very simple in that we had an objective to grow in excess of the rate of growth demanded by our parent company. However, that process has become less naive, more detailed and more structured as the business grows. I see planning as a process that goes on and on and on and becomes more complex and more refined.

He also made the following comment: 'Don't forget, not all strategies necessarily involve massive change. You can have a strategy to stay as you are.'

The director of marketing emphasized the dynamic nature of strategy in a growing business operating in a highly competitive environment: 'We have a strategy document that is concerned with developing market share and growth and is being continuously updated. The update is driven by the board. We have to make sure that we continue to refresh the strategy.'

The director of personnel commented that 'The longer-term strategy is developed basically by the board getting together and working its way through. We also share that plan with the senior management team.'

HR strategy

The managing director described their approach to developing the HR strategy as follows: 'Our HR strategy has to respond to our business needs, so we start with a business plan. We know we are going to grow at a certain rate. Then we do a skills audit and predict how many managers we are going to need. Out of this comes our HR development policy on skills training, leadership training and recruitment.'

The deputy managing director thought that the personnel director was basically responsible for developing their HR strategy: 'We all look at our business strategy and express a view on the people we need, but our HR director pulls it all together and interprets our ramblings into something coherent.'

However, in answering a question on how HR strategies were developed, the director of finance admitted that 'We probably have more HR policies than strategies because the strategies are there in a simple sense but not 100 per cent well articulated – for valid reasons: we are a growing business.'

The director of personnel referred to the way in which strategic initiatives were developed: 'First the personnel people meet and we bounce ideas about and seek ideas. Then if we have a new initiative we put it to the board for discussion.'

Loamshire Council

Loamshire Council is a district council that is generally recognized as being a very well-run and capable local authority. It is particularly good at dealing with the environment and, as the chief executive said, 'We tend to care so passionately about our environment that we focus an almost disproportionate amount of our resources on environmental issues.' He further commented that the critical success factors for the authority were meeting the perceived needs of the community, creating customer satisfaction with the services provided and, importantly, 'an overall appreciation of the effectiveness of members of staff and the contribution they make towards the organization as a whole'.

Corporate strategy

The following comments were made by the chief executive on how corporate strategy was developed:

We do not have a single document that says 'This is the Loamshire Council corporate strategy.' What we do have is three processes that run in parallel and together represent the corporate strategy. This comprises a *general strategy* for developing services, a *management strategy*, which concentrates on the managerial processes that we need to design to bring out the best in the organization, and the *key areas for achievement* document, which focuses on specific actions.

Strategies are developed by a top-down, bottom-up process. The members of the council, the policy makers, debate the strategic issues from which firm strategic proposals would develop. Individual members of staff are then given opportunities to contribute. A distinguishing feature of all our corporate strategy work has been the opportunity for widespread involvement in the process.

It is incredibly important that within an organization there is somebody who has the personal responsibility for monitoring, evaluating and reviewing the effectiveness of that organization. That strategic management role lies at the heart of the chief executive's responsibility.

The director of planning commented as follows on the process of strategic planning:

The reality is you choose directions and you move in particular directions; then all sorts of things happen that you can't possibly have conceived of, and you weave these into your strategy.

Strategy is rooted in the vision and the culture. Life's very complicated, there are no easy solutions, and you don't start at Go when you throw a six and proceed from there. You pick up a very complex jigsaw and you work through it. But the vision helps.

On how the top team operates the director of planning said that 'The things we bring to the team are personal characteristics as much as the management skills we all learn at various stages. The fact that we have a spectrum of personalities strengthens the team.'

HR strategy

The chief executive stated that:

Human resource strategy has got to be owned by the top management body within an organization. Their commitment must be absolute; otherwise it simply won't be applied in practice. Everything flows from the corporate strategies we have set down. It's about having a very strong focus on the overall effectiveness of the organization, its direction and how it's performing.

There is commitment to, and belief in, and respect for, individuals, and I think that these are very important factors in an organization.

When asked how HR strategies were developed the director of personnel replied:

Initially what I did was to list all the activities in which we were currently involved in personnel and sent a questionnaire to all the directors stating 'This is what we are doing' and asking: 'Do you want us to continue doing it? If so, do you want the same, or more, or less? Are we doing it well? Could we do it better? What are the things we are not doing that you think we ought to be doing?' The next thing I did was to have two open days in which I invited managers to come in and tell us what their perceptions of personnel were. And this confirmed our eagerness to get rid of duplication and delays in personnel matters. We were fast getting in the way and holding the whole process up. And that's where we got the agreement of the organization that empowerment should be our strategy.

On this strategy for empowerment, the director of technical services remarked: 'The positive aspects of the devolution of responsibility for personnel management is that it puts people management back where it should be.'

Megastores

Megastores is one of the country's largest and most successful high street retailers. It has a very powerful overriding commercial objective, to increase shareholder's value, and to do this by providing value-for-money products and delivering consistently high levels of customer service.

Business strategy

The managing director made the following observations about strategic management: 'Strategy is developing a route to better the business in the medium to long term. You cannot fully maximize the business opportunities unless you've got the proper management structure to create them. In business you have to look at the options available, make a decision and then drive that way.'

The approach to strategy formulation was described by the director of finance as follows:

Our strategy tends to be based on the resolution of issues. There is a base strategy and we continue to question whether that is the right thing to be going forward with. We have a strategic planning framework throughout the group. It's called value-based management (VBM), the fundamentals of which are to make sure that, whatever you do, you must maximize shareholder value. It provides us with a basis for looking at what we are doing and the resources we require that we've never had before.

He also commented, however, that 'We're highly profitable, but in turn we invest an awful lot in our people. We spend a lot of money on the training and development of people throughout the organization. It's probably one of our key differentiators.'

The director of stores gave these perspectives on the strategic planning process:

We have in place a formal business planning process in which we divide the planning into three levels. One is at business level, where we identify issues that we deal with as a company, the second level is product-market planning, and the third level is local market planning.

Our business strategy is formed through value-based management, which is a discipline for pulling everything together and ensures that decisions are made on the basis of their real value to the business rather than someone's strength of personality or hunch. This in itself required the involvement of all the directors in a more formal business planning process. Three or four years ago we worked more individually and now we work more as a team.

There are elements of our business that are incredibly value creating. There are others that are incredibly value destroying. The trick is to identify the ones that *are* value creating and funnel resources to them.

There are a number of blocks that make up our business strategy. The first is our overall objective. Against this we spin off a number of elements we call major initiatives. These are coordinated by our director of corporate planning, but it is the functional directors who are really charged with taking ownership of these objectives.

HR strategy

The comments made by the managing director and a number of other directors on the formulation of HR strategy are given below:

The biggest challenge will be to maintain our competitive advantage and to do what we need to maintain and continue to attract very high-calibre people.

(Managing director)

All we do in terms of training and human resource planning is directly linked to business improvement.

(Managing director)

The key differentiator on anything any company does is fundamentally the people, and I think that people tend to forget that they are the most important asset. Money is easy to get hold of; good people are not.

(Managing director)

The influence in terms of strategic direction must always be based on the key areas of marketing and operations.

(Director of finance)

We have to help the business achieve its objectives, and the HR strategy has to be very much tailored towards those objectives.

(Director of personnel)

When questioned on his approach to the development of personnel strategies the director of personnel replied:

I start with the top line, the four or five things that are the strategic platform for the company. I get my managers together to look at the implications. We then pull it together so that it is all derived from the original strategic platforms and then work top down and bottom up to get the amalgam of what we can achieve. This then feeds into the final operating plan so we can agree budgets.

Mercia Systems

Background

Mercia Systems is engaged in the business of precision engineering, including the development and manufacture of specialized optical, mechanical, electrical and electronic equipment primarily for defence purposes.

Two major factors have affected the company: first, the contraction in the defence industry and, second, the change in government policy from cost-plus contracting to competitive tendering. This compelled the company to develop an entirely new business strategy and to carry out a comprehensive re-engineering process.

Critical success factors

The managing director stated unequivocally that 'The things that are essential to an organization's success, any organization, not just this one, are the people. They are the common denominator throughout the organization.'

The critical success factors for Mercia Systems were defined as follows:

The one factor that drives us is technology know-how. This means we offer solutions, not products. That is really what we have to sell and it depends on people strength.

(Managing director)

We have a vision of what we want to be and are advancing more quickly than the rest of the competition. CIM [computer integrated manufacture] is at the heart of it. We have tackled MRPII [manufacturing requirements planning] as the first phase of CIM, and this means that we are faster than our competitors and are more likely to deliver on time than them.

(General manager)

We are characterized in the marketplace as a high-tech company with specific expertise in the field of optics and particularly electro-optics. We are known for the excellence of our technical solutions and the quality of our products. In the past we have been criticized for asking a premium price for high-technology products. Part of the message we are now getting across is that we can battle it out on value for money as well. People like working with us because they get straight answers to their questions, including 'We don't know' if we really don't know. So our basic competences are high technical quality and people with the skills needed to forge good relationships with customers.

(Marketing director)

Business strategy

Business strategy is stimulated and reviewed centrally by a business strategy group. The business is split into a number of sectors (three in Glasgow), and each sector submits its business plan to the strategy group. This is a simple three-page summary that describes the broad objectives of their business sector, discusses the key competitive factors affecting it and sets out specific short- to medium-term objectives, which are then translated into an operating plan. The plans look at a horizon of 10 years, but for practical purposes there is a rolling three-year budget. This means that besides looking at the immediate budget the two key questions asked are, as the general manager put it: 'Where are you going to be in three years' time? What are you doing now to get better?' And this, he said, 'is a very demanding discipline'.

The marketing director explained the approach as follows:

The key to the business planning process is that it has to be a linked story from the top to the bottom of the company, and MRPII [manufacturing requirements planning] is part of the vehicle for doing that. Our director of strategic planning works with the technical director to involve and guide the board on the overall strategic direction of the company. This is communicated as the strategic vision. Working from that, my role is to work with the group directors to evolve strategies for each of the businesses we have chosen to be in. These are then reviewed and agreed by the executive and a strategic development group. One of the roles of that group is to check that our activities relate to and support the strategy established by the executive. If they do not, this may not be because they are wrong, and we may have to go back and review the strategy.

The formulation of business strategy is very much a team effort. As the managing director said: 'I tell all the top executive people, including the personnel and finance directors, that they are directors first and foremost and all must make a contribution to strategic planning.'

The lead may be taken by the managing director and the strategic team, of which the personnel director is a member, but the heads of the business groups make a major and continuing contribution. The broad thrust of the strategy as a means of realizing the vision is quite clear, but it is in a constant state of evolution, reacting as necessary in response to changing situations but also proactively anticipating new opportunities.

Personnel strategies

The overall approach to the formulation of personnel strategies was summarized by the managing director as follows: 'The main thing we have to do is to ensure that we have the right core technologies and the right competences within the company to achieve the vision and strategy.'

The general manager commented that:

> Within the board one of the things that is constantly reviewed is human resource strategy. We have the long-term view of the type of organization we believe we need as a technology company and we have evolutionary plans of how we are going to get there. In the early stages we had a very strong functional organization; our evolution process now involves the development of problem-solving teams, which are set up at a high standard to encourage getting it right first time. In manufacturing we have mixed-discipline teams with a team leader and a much flatter structure than we used to have. We have two pilot projects where research and development engineers are part of the team on the shop floor, with a common team leader. The eventual aim is for all engineering and manufacturing to be organized in this way. The next step is to develop product families in which business generation and sales are brought into the team as well. So the team leaders almost become general managers.

The marketing director pointed out that the personnel strategy was 'clearly established in the planning process and it had hard objectives in the same way as the business strategy'.

The personnel director explained that business strategy defines what has to be done to achieve success and that personnel strategy must complement it, bearing in mind that one of the critical success factors for the company is its ability to attract and retain the best people. Personnel strategy must help to ensure that Mercia Systems is a best-practice company. This implies that 'The personnel strategy must be in line with what is best in industry and this may mean visiting four or five different companies, looking at what they are doing and taking a bit from one and a bit from another and moulding them together to form the strategy.'

Welland Water

Welland Water is a large water company operating, as pointed out by the managing director, 'in a monopolistic situation providing a service that is absolutely fundamental to life'. But he also stated that 'we recognize that our organization must not abuse that situation and that we must implant in the company values that would be appropriate in a competitive environment'.

He went on to say:

> We can demonstrate that the services we are giving our customers are improving dramatically, year on year. We have an ongoing commitment to involve our customers – we were the first water company to actually prepare an annual report for them. We carry out frequent tracking research, which shows that our customers' perceptions of us are improving, on occasions despite a contrary trend in the national water industry. But the critical success factor that allows all this to happen is the level of employee satisfaction and commitment we have, because without that we can't achieve any of the other things. And we know about this because we get consultants to carry out periodical employee surveys, which we discuss with everyone.

Business strategy

The managing director described the approach to formulating business strategy as follows:

> Our strategic approach is very simple. It is summarized in our vision statement: we aim to provide the level of services our customers demand at a level of charges that our customers would see as acceptable. Our business strategies are formed essentially from top-down setting of the parameters and then bottom-up preparation of business plans in which all our people are involved. They prepare all their own business plans, which reflect the top-down constraints, and because they are preparing them that automatically buys their commitment to them.
>
> Our best ideas for policies and strategies come from the people who carry out the work. We don't have people locked into little rooms, thinking 'What's the next strategic move for the business?'
>
> What you need is people who are in tune with what's happening throughout the organization – who are listening, talking, picking up all the ideas. What we try to do is to capture all that knowledge, all those initiatives, all that expertise, and reflect that in the way we take the business forward.
>
> I like to talk about getting values in place rather than constructing strategies.

The finance director explained the significance of the vision statement in developing business strategies: 'The company developed a vision statement that encompasses the key forward-looking strategy over a period of time but without timescales having been set down. This has set the guidelines for future initiatives, and any such initiative in the rolling five-year business plan is judged on whether it fits in with that vision.'

HR strategy

The managing director made the point that 'The only human resource strategy you really need is the tangible expression of values and the implementation of values. Unless you get the human resource values right you can forget all the rest.'

The finance director commented that 'There's a lot of interaction, prior to and during the top board discussion, which tends to be concerned with culturally based issues and the way we manage people.'

And the director of operations indicated that the organization developed its HR strategy 'through evolution: it's an aggregation of things that have come together, not necessarily in the right order'.

The approach to developing HR strategy was described by the head of personnel as follows:

> In our original HR strategy we tried to encompass the emerging values and principles that we felt should determine how we should conduct our business in terms of people. HR strategies come from the ideas we share together and the problems and issues that managers are working on. It's very much a team effort, working with line colleagues in whatever they do. I use e-mail to flash ideas round to groups of managers and thus build up draft policy papers. E-mail is a very powerful device for getting ideas back rapidly.

Comments

In all the organizations referred to above:

- ▌ there is a well-defined corporate or business strategy, although the extent to which it is formalized varies;
- ▌ HR strategy is seen as part of the business strategy;
- ▌ HR strategy or policy issues *appeared* to be of interest to all members of the board and, contrary to popular opinion, that includes the finance director.

THE CONTENT OF HR STRATEGIES

The rhetoric behind the concepts of human resource management, strategic management and strategic HRM has an inspiring ring about it, but does anything actually happen? And if so what does it look like? Process is important, but content and action are also required. In the research conducted by Armstrong and Long (1994) it was assumed that the basis of any approach an organization used to develop and implement HR strategies would be the philosophy of influential members of the top team on managing people. The content and programmes of the organizations covered by the research were examined to identify what was contained in their HR strategies and how they were implementing them. This was done under the headings of: macro, corporate issues such as vision and mission, organization, performance, quality and customer care, commitment, and the introduction of new technology; and the more specific HR strategy areas of resourcing, learning, development and training, reward, and employee relations.

Philosophy on managing people

The philosophy on managing people is a broad strategic issue associated with management style, and it is one that may never be articulated and so often remains on a 'taken for granted' basis like other manifestations of corporate culture. The philosophy may lead to a 'hard HRM' or a 'soft HRM' approach or a combination of the two as described in Chapter 1.

But to adapt a common if somewhat inadequate definition of corporate culture, strategic HRM is about 'the way things should be done about here in the future'. Questions can be asked about the traditional or underlying philosophy, the extent to which it is still relevant, and the directions in which it might usefully change.

The philosophy of the managing director of Megastores on managing people was expressed as follows:

> There is immense strength and talent in any body of people numbering 50,000, and we are negligent if we don't tap that resource as far as we possibly can... The contribution of our managers to added value is immense because they are people managers... They are not managing systems, they are not managing machinery and they are not managing shops. You can't manage a shop; you manage people within a shop.
>
> I have always advocated the employment of the highest calibre of people we can find, and I think we've got that. We are in the vanguard of retailing. Our net-profit-to-sales ratio is about the highest in the high street, and in profit terms we are growing at a faster rate than the market. The biggest challenge will be to maintain that competitive advantage and to do that we need to maintain and continue to attract very high-calibre people.

CORPORATE ISSUES

Vision and mission

In the broadest terms strategic HRM is concerned with the people implications of top management's vision of the future of the organization and the mission it is there to fulfil. HR strategies, like those of all the other functions, are there to support the realization of the vision and mission of the organization and the achievement of its goals.

The personnel director at Mercia Systems made the following comment about vision and strategy: 'The first thing is that the organization has to know where it is going. That is why it needs a vision. It has to know why it exists and who its customers are. This leads to the development of strategies, which in turn lead to action plans. The plans follow three lanes: systems, processes and people.'

Two of the other functional directors at Mercia Systems commented on the significance of vision and a sense of purpose or mission:

> I would put it in a single word, which is vision. If you can create a vision and communicate it to people you can release a colossal current of energy. Communication and vision mean education and training, and I am one of the operational guys who believe that whatever you are currently spending on education and training you start by doubling it.

> What contributes most to success is a clear sense of purpose and definition of where you are trying to get to. Unless you have a top team with a clear and unified understanding of purpose and direction it can be difficult to cascade it throughout the organization.

The managing director of Welland Water commented that 'We look at our vision for the company and we say: "How do we maximize the contribution that our people can make to achieving that vision?"'

Organization

HR strategy may address such issues as structure, teamworking, performance or quality and customer care.

Structure

The managing director of ABC Distribution said that 'I do not see any difference between the HR strategy and the business strategy on organization because we evolve our organization to reflect where the business is going.'

As the managing director of Megastores said, 'You cannot fully maximize business opportunities unless you have the proper management structure to create them.'

Teamworking

At Mercia Systems the background to the work on team building was the demolition of traditional hierarchies over the last two to three years. In manufacturing and engineering there are never more than three layers between team members and the director. In 80 per cent of the engineering teams there are now only two layers – the team manager and the engineering manager. It is believed that these changes have had far-reaching effects on flexibility and performance and have contributed significantly to the achievement of better coordination in manufacturing and engineering.

Performance

A performance strategy will be based on an analysis of the critical success factors and the performance levels reached in relation to them. Steps can then be agreed as to what needs to be done to improve performance by training, development, reorganization, the development of performance management processes, some form of business process re-engineering, or simply 'taking cost out of the business'. This is how a cost reduction strategy works in one of the key divisions of ABC Distribution as described by the managing director:

> We know that over the next three years we have to take more than £10 million worth of cost out of the business. So our personnel director sits down with the business head of the division and they identify the areas we need to focus on. It could be productivity enhancement; it could be changing work practices; it could be making sure that we have no anomalies round the depots in terms of payment; it could even be taking tea breaks out. A three-year strategy is agreed, targets are set and then they get on with it.

The approach at Loamshire Council was described by the director of personnel as follows: 'We have a general strategy of performance measurement and management from which grew our performance appraisal system, which has worked extremely well. We spent a lot of time ensuring that people understood that this was a development process and it was about not just their competence but also the ability of the organization to achieve what it wants to achieve.'

The strategy for improving performance at Megastores involves the use of a performance management system, which was introduced, as the director of personnel explained, 'because we didn't have any mechanism through which we could run the business through the people'. He went on to say: 'Line management own it totally. It's not a personnel system; it's a line management system for running the business.'

The director of personnel for Megastores also made the following comments on performance strategies:

> We set out to understand the differences between successful and less successful performance within the organization and we call those our competency frameworks. By developing these frameworks we have educated the whole of our line management throughout the organization into how to think about their people in a much wider sense. Our key HR strategy question is: 'How do we actually get the people to deliver what the business requires?'

The process of performance improvement could mean, as Mercia Systems' marketing director put it, 'going through a lot of effort to ensure that we have the correct level of performance in what we do and underpinning this with financial and commercial stability'.

Mercia Systems successfully used a functional analysis process, which, as described by the personnel director, was carried out as shown in Figure 7.1.

At Welland Water, the head of personnel thought that:

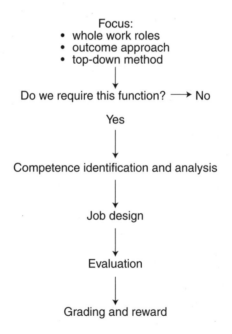

Figure 7.1 Methodology of occupational analysis to meet the company's business needs

Performance improvement lies not so much in creating the hard issues at the bottom line but on creating an environment within which people will accept change and cooperate in different methods of working. And I believe our partnership approach does create such an environment, one in which we can manage change successfully and which encourages people to accept new responsibilities and acquire new skills.

The majority of the organizations covered by the research had installed performance management processes in which the emphasis was on performance improvement and development and not reward. The scheme in Mercia Systems emphasized the new priorities of involvement, teamwork and self-development as well as more standard measures.

Quality and customer care

Quality, which in essence means customer satisfaction, is generally recognized today as the key to the achievement of competitive advantage. Innovation and cost reduction are still important but they are to no avail if, ultimately, customers reject the product because it does not meet their expectations. Quality is achieved through people and, in accordance with a basic HRM principle, investment in people is a prerequisite for achieving high-quality standards.

A strategy for total quality is a true HRM strategy in the sense that it is owned and delivered by management. It should therefore be built into their business strategy as it is, for example, for Mercia Systems.

The chief executive of Loamshire Council said that 'We have a performance appraisal system and one area that we are particularly keen should be dealt with as part of that process is the contribution of the individual to our customer care standards.'

At Mercia Systems, the personnel director stated that, in pursuit of their goal of world-class performance, personnel strategy must help to ensure that they are a best-practice company. An important aspect of this strategy 'is to educate everyone to build quality into every job, aiming to convey to people that if you get it right first time they will be saving a lot of unnecessary work'.

ACHIEVING INTEGRATION

The integration of HR and business strategies is seen by some commentators as a main distinguishing feature of strategic HRM. Doubts have been cast by a number of commentators such as Storey (1993) on the extent to which such integration does take place, often on the grounds that integration is not an issue when there are no corporate strategies. This was not the case in any of the eight organizations referred to earlier. In all but two of them the HR strategies, in Walker's (1992) terms, were fully integrated, while in these cases the strategies were 'aligned'.

As the managing director of ABC Distribution pointed out: 'Our HR strategy has to respond to our business strategy. The challenge for HR is to look at all the areas that they encompass and make sure they are integrated into the main plan.' But he admitted that 'One of the problems this company used to have up to a few years ago was that HR strategy was seen as something completely separate from the corporate strategy. What we have tried to do in the past few years is to make them one and the same thing.'

The director of personnel of ABC Distribution recognized that 'The development of HR strategies should be shared more widely with the business controllers. If we don't do that we run the risk of not developing the consistent themes we need to have.' But the director of finance was positive that 'In terms of performance improvement the business and HR strategies are very closely linked. Productivity is a major area and the HR implications of pursuing these policies are critical.'

These, incidentally, were not the only positive contributions from finance directors. It was found by Armstrong and Long (1994) that, without exception, the eight finance directors we interviewed were all fully aware of the significance of the HR perspective for their organizations, although they were obviously concerned with financial performance and budgets.

In Loamshire Council, the approach to integration as described by the director of personnel was simply to get the top team together and ask them: 'What are the real strategies that will help the organization and its functioning?' And the director of planning for the authority commented on the important integrating role of the director of personnel as follows:

> In the old days, the personnel manager was not a member of the management team, and I got used to a culture where personnel advice was not really part of strategic direction. And any debate there may have been at the corporate level came out in the wash. It was not led by someone like our director of personnel. She is now on a par with the rest of us in terms of status and contribution and she brings the whole of the human resource angle into the debate.

And in reply to the question 'How well are corporate and HR strategies integrated?' the director of technical services for the authority said: 'The short answer is that they are inextricably linked... You cannot do anything without having worked through the human resource implications and it's all about better performance by teams and individuals.'

The approach of Megastores was described by the director of stores as follows:

The starting point is the operating plan emerging from and contributing to the business plan. There is only a certain level of change we can cope with, and what we have is a funnel of brilliant ideas and strategies, but they all end up in the stores. So we only commit to a plan we can deliver, and we identify the levels of change that we can manage and calculate how much time the stores have to implement it. That is fed into the planning process so that it becomes realistic. The human resource strategy is integral to the process; it's not linked.

At Mercia Systems integration was not an issue. As explained by the marketing director:

We do not think of ourselves as having a human resource strategy per se. We just see it as one aspect of the overall business strategy. From what I have observed going on in the business I find it quite difficult to separate a strand of activity which I would call HR strategy because it is so integral to everything which is going on… HR strategy is effectively a part of the overall vision.

He gave the example of the technical director, who is developing technical route maps, and the personnel function, which is working with technical management to produce forecasts as a basis for finding and developing the right people with the right skills. His own role is to explain the nature of the competences required in the business groups, including business management, programme management and sales and marketing: 'Only by understanding these can we equip ourselves for the future.'

The director of finance for Welland Water pointed out that 'The HR side is a fundamental part of the business planning process, and it's not something you just bolt on somewhere along the way. There's a lot of interaction, prior to and during the top board discussion, which tends to be concerned with culturally based issues and the way we manage people.'

On the basis of these comments integration is most likely to be achieved when:

▌ there are well-articulated corporate or business strategies operating in the context of a clear mission;

▌ there is a powerful driving force in the shape of commitment to certain values and overall strategies for change;

▌ the chief executive or managing director recognizes the contribution that people make to increasing added value and achieving competitive advantage and ensures that people issues are fully taken into account *at the time corporate or business strategies are being prepared*;

▌ the other members of the top team generally share the views of their chief executive on the added value that can be created by considering HR and corporate/business issues simultaneously;

▌ the HR director is capable of making a full contribution to the formulation of corporate/business strategies as well as those relating to people;

▌ the views of the HR director are listened to, respected and acted upon;

▌ unions are involved in developing change strategies on a partnership basis;

▌ HR strategies relate to the critical success factors of the organization and the impact high-quality and committed people can make on the delivery of the results the organization is expected to achieve.

WHAT ARE THE MOST CHARACTERISTIC FEATURES OF STRATEGIC HRM IN ACTION?

To summarize, the most characteristic features of strategic HRM in action in the case study organizations mentioned above were that:

▌ a clear and purposeful corporate or business strategy exists;

▌ the HR strategies in most cases are fully integrated and owned by the whole of the top management team;

▌ the HR strategies are very much concerned with developing the organization and the people in it.

Most if not all of the organizations could be described as 'unitarist' in their approach (ie they believed in the commonality of the interests of management and employees), and they are all striving to develop a 'commitment-orientated' culture. But in many cases they have still taken pains to involve the trade unions.

Part 3

HR strategies

8

Human capital management strategy

Human capital management (HCM) is concerned with obtaining, analysing and reporting on data that inform the direction of value-adding people management strategy. An HCM strategy is therefore closely associated with strategic HRM.

The defining characteristic of HCM is the use of metrics to guide an approach to managing people that regards them as assets. It emphasizes that competitive advantage is achieved by strategic investments in those assets through employee engagement and retention, talent management and learning and development programmes. HCM provides a bridge between HR and business strategy. It provides the basis for 'evidence-based human resource management'.

The Accounting for People Task Force report (2003) stated that HCM involves the systematic analysis, measurement and evaluation of how people policies and practices create value. The report defined HCM as 'an approach to people management that treats it as a high level strategic issue rather than an operational matter "to be left to the HR people"'. The task force expressed the view that HCM 'has been under-exploited as a way of gaining competitive edge'. As John Sunderland, task force member and executive chairman of Cadbury Schweppes plc, commented, 'An organization's success is the product of its people's competence. That link between people and performance should be made visible and available to all stakeholders.'

Nalbantian *et al* (2004) highlight the purposeful measurement aspect of HCM. They define human capital as the 'stock of accumulated knowledge, skills, experience, creativity and other relevant workforce attributes' and suggest that human capital management involves 'putting into place the metrics to measure the value of these attributes and using that knowledge to effectively manage the organization'.

HCM is sometimes defined more broadly without the emphasis on measurement, and this approach makes it almost indistinguishable from strategic HRM. Chatzkel (2004) states that 'Human capital management is an integrated effort to manage and develop human capabilities to achieve significantly higher levels of performance.' And Kearns (2005) describes HCM as the 'total development of human potential expressed as organizational value'. He believes that 'HCM is about creating value through people' and that it is 'a people development philosophy, but the only development that means anything is that which is translated into value'.

AIMS OF HUMAN CAPITAL MANAGEMENT

The four fundamental objectives of HCM are:

1. to determine the impact of people on the business and their contribution to value;
2. to demonstrate that HR practices produce value for money in terms, for example, of return on investment;
3. to provide guidance on future HR and business strategies;
4. to provide data that will inform strategies and practices designed to improve the effectiveness of people management in the organization.

THE LINK BETWEEN HCM AND BUSINESS STRATEGY

It is often asserted that HCM and business strategy are closely linked and that an HCM approach provides guidance on both HR and business strategy. For example:

▌ By linking good HR practice and strategic management to human capital measurement, firms are able to make a number of better-informed decisions that will help to ensure long-term business success (Scarborough and Elias, 2002).

▌ The aim is to have a 'robust people strategy mapped to the business strategy' (Manocha, 2005).

▌ The prime purpose of human capital management is to establish 'an employment proposition that links the work of employees to strategy and profits' (Donkin, 2005).

The issue is to determine what this link is and how to make it work. A bland statement that HCM informs HR strategy, which in turn informs business strategy, tells us nothing about what is involved in practice. If we are not careful we are saying no more than that all business strategic plans for innovation, growth and price/cost leadership depend on people for their implementation. This is not a particularly profound or revealing statement and is in the same category as the discredited cliché 'Our people are our greatest asset.' We must try to be more specific; otherwise we are only doing things – more training, succession planning, performance management, performance-related pay and so on – in the hope rather than the expectation that they will improve business results.

One way of being more specific is to use HCM assessments of the impact of HR practices on performance to justify these practices and improve the likelihood that they will work. The future of HCM as a strategic management process largely depends on getting this done.

A second way of specifying the link is to explore in more detail the people implications of business strategy and, conversely, the business implications of HR strategy. This can be done by analysing the elements of the business strategy and the business drivers and deciding on the HR supporting activities and HCM data required, as illustrated in Table 8.1.

A third, and potentially the most productive way of linking HR and business strategy, is to relate business results to HR practices to determine how they can best contribute to improving performance.

DEVELOPING A HUMAN CAPITAL MANAGEMENT STRATEGY

The programme for introducing human capital management is illustrated in Figure 8.1.

The development programme starts with a definition of the aims of the strategy, for example to:

▌ obtain, analyse and report on data that inform the direction of HR strategies and processes;

▌ inform the development of business strategy;

Table 8.1 Analysis of business strategy and business drivers

	Content	HR Supporting Activities	Supporting Data Required
Business Strategy	Growth – revenue, profit. Maximize shareholder value. Growth through acquisitions or mergers. Growth in production or servicing facilities. Product development. Market development. Price/cost leadership.	Human resource planning. Talent management. Skills development. Targeted recruitment. Retention policies. Leadership development.	Workforce composition. Attrition rates. Skills audit. Outcome of recruitment campaigns. Learning and development activity levels. Outcome of leadership surveys.
Business Drivers	Innovation. Maximize added value. Productivity. Customer service. Quality. Satisfy stakeholders – investors, shareholders, employees, elected representatives.	Talent management. Skills development. Total reward management. Performance management. Develop high-performance working. Enhance motivation, engagement and commitment. Leadership development.	Balanced scorecard data. Added-value ratios (eg added value per employee, added value per pound of employment cost). Productivity ratios (eg sales revenue per employee, units produced or serviced per employee). Outcomes of general employee opinion survey and other surveys covering engagement and commitment, leadership, reward management and performance management. Analysis of competence level assessments. Analysis of performance management assessments. Analysis of customer surveys. Analysis of outcomes of total quality programmes. Return on investment from training activities. Internal promotion rate. Succession planning coverage.

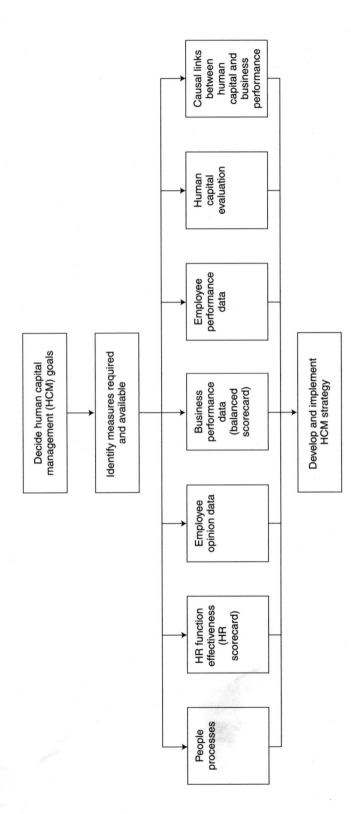

Figure 8.1 Developing an HCM strategy

▮ use measurements to prove that superior HRM strategies and processes deliver superior results;

▮ reinforce the belief that HRM strategies and processes create value through people;

▮ determine the impact of people on business results;

▮ assess the value of the organization's human capital;

▮ improve the effectiveness of HR;

▮ provide data on the performance of the organization's human capital for the operating and financial report;

▮ demonstrate that HR processes provide value for money.

The programme continues with the identification of possible measures and how they can be used, as set out in Table 8.2.

The analysis of possible measures leads to the development of a strategy for introducing and using them. It is often best to start with information that is readily available and extend the range of data as experience is gained. And it is important to remember that it is the quality of the information that counts, not the quantity.

Table 8.2 Possible HCM measures and their use

Possible Measures	Possible Use – Analysis Leading to Action
Workforce composition – gender, race, age, full-time, part-time.	Analyse the extent of diversity. Assess the implications of a preponderance of employees in different age groups, eg extent of losses through retirement. Assess the extent to which the organization is relying on part-time staff.
Length of service distribution.	Indicate level of success in retaining employees. Indicate preponderance of long- or short-serving employees. Enable analyses of performance of more experienced employees to be assessed.
Skills analysis and assessment – graduates, professionally or technically qualified, skilled workers.	Assess skill levels against requirements. Indicate where steps have to be taken to deal with shortfalls.
Attrition – employee turnover rates for different categories of management and employees.	Indicate areas where steps have to be taken to increase retention rates. Provide a basis for assessing levels of commitment.
Attrition – cost of.	Support business case for taking steps to reduce attrition.
Absenteeism and sickness rates.	Identify problems and need for more effective attendance management policies.
Average number of vacancies as a percentage of total workforce.	Identify potential shortfall problem areas.
Total payroll costs (pay and benefits).	Provide data for productivity analysis.

Possible Measures	**Possible Use – Analysis Leading to Action**
Compa-ratio – actual rates of pay as a percentage of policy rates.	Enable control to be exercised over management of pay structure.
Percentage of employees in different categories of contingent pay or payment-by-result schemes.	Demonstrate the extent to which the organization believes that pay should be related to contribution.
Total pay review increases for different categories of employees as a percentage of pay.	Compare actual with budgeted payroll increase costs. Benchmark pay increases.
Average bonuses or contingent pay awards as a percentage of base pay for different categories of managers and employees.	Analyse cost of contingent pay. Compare actual and budgeted increases.Benchmark increases.
Outcome of equal pay reviews.	Reveal pay gap between male and female employees.
Personal development plans completed as a percentage of employees.	Indicate level of learning and development activity.
Training hours per employee.	Indicate actual amount of training activity (note that this does not reveal the quality of training achieved or its impact).
Percentage of managers taking part in formal management development programmes.	Indicate level of learning and development activity.
Internal promotion rate (percentage of promotions filled from within).	Indicate extent to which talent management programmes are successful.
Succession planning coverage (percentage of managerial jobs for which successors have been identified).	Indicate extent to which talent management programmes are successful.
Percentage of employees taking part in formal performance reviews.	Indicate level of performance management activity.
Distribution of performance ratings by category of staff and department.	Indicate inconsistencies, questionable distributions and trends in assessments.
Accident severity and frequency rates.	Assess health and safety programmes.
Cost savings and revenue increases resulting from employee suggestion schemes.	Measure the value created by employees.
Measures of impact of HR practices.	Evaluation of effectiveness.

CONCLUSIONS: THE ROLE OF HUMAN CAPITAL MANAGEMENT STRATEGY

The whole area of human capital management presents both an opportunity and a challenge: an opportunity to recognize people as an asset that contributes directly to organizational performance, and a challenge to develop the skills necessary to identify, analyse and communicate that contribution and ensure it is recognized in business decision making. By developing strategies to generate better and more accurate information on human capital and communicating this information both internally and externally, organizations will not only improve their business decision making but also enable stakeholders to make more accurate assessments about the long-term future performance of the organization. There is evidence of a growing demand, from the investment community in particular, for better information to explain intangible value. Many organizations are beginning to understand that, in an increasingly knowledge-intensive environment, the key to good management lies in understanding the levers that can be manipulated to change employee behaviour and develop commitment and engagement. This in turn encourages individuals to deliver discretionary behaviour or willingly share their knowledge and skills to achieve organizational goals.

A human capital management strategy that includes the systematic collection and analysis of human capital data can help managers to begin to understand factors that will have a direct impact on the people they manage. It can also help executives to understand and identify areas in which there are issues regarding the effective management of staff and to design management development programmes to address these.

9

High-performance strategy

A high-performance strategy sets out the intentions of the organization on how it can achieve competitive advantage by improving performance through people. The aim is to support the achievement of the organization's strategic objectives. This aim can be put into effect by means of high-performance work systems (HPWS) as described in this chapter. Becker *et al* (2001) have stated that the aim of such systems is to develop a 'high-performance perspective in which HR and other executives view HR as a system embedded within the larger system of the firm's strategy implementation'. As Nadler (1989) commented, they are deliberately introduced in order to improve organizational, financial and operational performance.

High-performance work systems are also known as high-performance work practices (Sung and Ashton, 2005). Thompson and Heron (2005) refer to them as high-performance work organizations, which 'invest in the skills and abilities of employees, design work in ways that enable employee collaboration in problem-solving, and provide incentives to motivate workers to use their discretionary effort'. There is much common ground between the practices included in high-performance, high-commitment and high-involvement work systems, as described in Chapter 4. Sung and Ashton (2005) note that:

In some cases high performance work practices are called 'high commitment practices' (Walton, 1985) or 'high involvement management' (Lawler, 1986).

More recently they have been termed 'high performance organizations' (Lawler *et al* 1998; Ashton and Sung, 2002) or 'high-involvement' work practices (Wood *et al*, 2001). Whilst these studies are referring to the same general phenomena the use of different 'labels' has undoubtedly added to the confusion.

HIGH-PERFORMANCE WORK SYSTEM DEFINED

As defined by Appelbaum *et al* (2000), high-performance work systems are composed of practices that can facilitate employee involvement, skill enhancement and motivation. Research conducted by Armitage and Keeble-Allen (2007) indicated that people management basics formed the foundation of high-performance working. They identified three themes underpinning the HPWS concept:

1. an open and creative culture that is people-centred and inclusive, where decision taking is communicated and shared through the organization;
2. investment in people through education and training, loyalty, inclusiveness and flexible working;
3. measurable performance outcomes such as benchmarking and setting targets, as well as innovation through processes and best practice.

Sung and Ashton (2005) defined what they call high-performance work practices as a set of 35 complementary work practices covering three broad areas: high-employee-involvement work practices, human resource practices, and reward and commitment practices. They refer to them as 'bundles' of practices.

CHARACTERISTICS OF A HIGH-PERFORMANCE WORK SYSTEM

A high-performance work system is described by Becker and Huselid (1998) as an 'internally consistent and coherent HRM system that is focused on solving operational problems and implementing the firm's competitive strategy'. They suggest that such a system 'is the key to the acquisition, motivation and development of the underlying intellectual assets that can be a source of sustained competitive advantage'. This is because it:

▌ links the firm's selection and promotion decisions to validated competency models;

▋ develops strategies that provide timely and effective support for the skills demanded by the firm's strategy implementation;

▋ enacts compensation and performance management policies that attract, retain and motivate high-performance employees.

As described by Appelbaum *et al* (2000) an HPWS is 'generally associated with workshop practices that raise the levels of trust within workplaces and increase workers' intrinsic reward from work, and thereby enhance organizational commitment'.

Nadler and Gerstein (1992) have characterized an HPWS as a way of thinking about organizations. It can play an important role in strategic human resource management by helping to achieve a 'fit' between information, technology, people and work.

COMPONENTS OF AN HPWS

Descriptions of high-performance systems include lists of desirable practices and therefore embody the notion of 'best practice' or the 'universalistic' approach described in Chapter 3. Lists vary considerably, as is shown in the selection set out in Table 9.1. Gephart (1995) notes that research has not clearly identified any single set of high-performance practices. And Sung and Ashton (2005) comment: 'It would be wrong to seek one magic list.' It all depends on the context.

However, Ashton and Sung (2002) noted that the practices may be more effective when they are grouped together in 'bundles'. For example, the isolated use of quality circles is not as effective as when the practice is supported by wider employee involvement or empowerment practices.

IMPACT OF HIGH-PERFORMANCE WORK SYSTEMS

A considerable number of studies as summarized below have been conducted that demonstrate that the impact of high-performance work systems is positive. A more negative study is also summarized.

US Department of Labor (1993)

In a survey of 700 organizations the US Department of Labor found that firms that used innovative human resource practices show a significantly higher level of shareholder and gross return on capital.

Table 9.1   Lists of HR practices in high-performance work systems

US Department of Labor (1993)	Appelbaum *et al* (2000)	Sung and Ashton (2005)	Thompson and Heron (2005)
Careful and extensive systems for recruitment, selection and training.	Work is organized to permit front-line workers to participate in decisions that alter organizational routines.	High-involvement work practices, eg self-directed teams, quality circles, and sharing of or access to company information.	Information sharing.
Formal systems for sharing information with employees.	Workers require more skills to do their jobs successfully, and many of these skills are firm-specific.	Human resource practices, eg sophisticated recruitment processes, performance appraisals, work redesign and mentoring.	Sophisticated recruitment.
Clear job design.			Formal induction programme.
High-level participation processes.			Five or more days of off-the-job training in the last year.
Monitoring of attitudes.	Workers experience greater autonomy over their job tasks and methods of work.		Semi- or totally autonomous work teams; continuous improvement teams; problem-solving groups.
Performance appraisals.	Incentive pay motivates workers to extend extra effort on developing skills.	Reward and commitment practices, eg various financial rewards, family-friendly policies, job rotation and flexi-hours.	Interpersonal skill development.
Properly functioning grievance procedures.			Performance feedback.
Promotion and compensation schemes that provide for the recognition and reward of high-performing employees.	Employment security provides front-line workers with a long-term stake in the company and a reason to invest in its future.		Involvement – works council, suggestion scheme, opinion survey.
			Team-based rewards, employee share ownership scheme, profit-sharing scheme.

Jeffrey King (1995)

Jeffrey King cites a survey of Fortune 1000 companies in the United States revealing that 60 per cent of those using at least one practice increasing the responsibility of employees in the business process reported that the result was an increase in productivity, while 70 per cent reported an improvement in quality.

He examined the impact of the use of one practice. A study of 155 manufacturing firms showed that those that had introduced a formal training programme experienced a 19 per cent larger rise in productivity over three years than firms that had not introduced a training programme. Research in the use of gainsharing in 112 manufacturing firms revealed that defect and downtime rates fell 23 per cent in the first year after the approach was introduced. His review of 29 studies on the effects of workplace participation on productivity indicated that 14 had a positive effect on productivity, only two had negative effects and the rest were inconclusive.

However, he noted that such work practices may have only a limited effect unless they are elements of a coherent work system. Further research examined changes over time in 222 firms and found that these and other practices were associated with even greater productivity when implemented together in systems.

He concluded that the evidence suggests that it is the use of comprehensive systems of work practices in firms that is most closely associated with stronger firm performance. Yet he noted that 'the nature of the relationship between high performance work practices and productivity is not clear'.

Arup Varma, Richard Beatty, Craig Schneier and David Ulrich (1999)

A survey of 39 organizations was conducted to examine the antecedents, design and effectiveness of high-performance initiatives. Results indicated that HPWSs are primarily initiated by strong firms that are seeking to become stronger. First and foremost, firms reported that in general their HPWS:

▍ had a significant impact on financial performance;
▍ created a positive culture change in the organization (eg cooperation and innovation);
▍ created higher degrees of job satisfaction among employees;
▍ positively influenced the way in which work was designed;
▍ led to marked improvement in communication processes within the organization.

In particular, the use of team-based and non-financial rewards was closely related to improved performance, as was rewarding people for improving their competencies.

Harvie Ramsay, Dora Scholarios and Bill Harley (2000)

The aim of this research was to explore linkages from HPWS practices to employee outcomes and via these to organizational performance. They refer to the existence of a 'black box', meaning that while the introduction of an HPWS may be associated with improved performance no researchers have yet established how this happens.

Their research was based on data from the UK 1998 Workplace Employee Relations Survey. They commented that 'the widely held view that positive performance outcomes from HPWS flow via positive employee outcomes has been shown to be highly questionable', a finding that ran counter to most if not all other studies. They admit that their analysis was 'perhaps too simplistic to capture the complex reality of the implementation and operation of HPWS', but they note, realistically, that 'there are major limitations to the strategic management of labour which severely constrain the potential for innovative approaches to be implemented successfully'.

Eileen Appelbaum, Thomas Bailey, Peter Berg and Arne Kalleberg (2000)

A multifaceted research design was used by the authors in their study of the impact of HPWSs. This included management interviews, the collection of plant performance and data surveys of workers on their experiences with workshop practices. Nearly 4,400 employees were surveyed and 44 manufacturing facilities were visited.

The findings of the research in industry were that:

▌ in the steel industry HPWSs produced a string of positive effects on performance, for example substantial increases in uptime;
▌ in the apparel industry the introduction of a 'module system' (ie group piecework rates linked to quality as well as quantity rather than individual piecework, plus multiskilling) dramatically speeded up throughput times, meeting consumer demands for fast delivery;
▌ in the medical electronics and imaging industry those using an HPWS ranked highly on eight diverse indicators of financial performance and production efficiency and quality.

The impact of HPWS on individual workers was to enhance:

▌ trust by sharing control and encouraging participation;
▌ intrinsic rewards because workers are challenged to be creative and use their skills and knowledge – intrinsic rewards are most likely to be enhanced where the role provides a reasonable degree of discretion and autonomy;
▌ organizational commitment through opportunity to participate, and incentives that make people feel that organizational relationships are beneficial for them;
▌ job satisfaction because of participation, perception of fairness in pay and adequate resources to do jobs (inadequate resources are a cause of dissatisfaction, as is working in an unsafe or unclean environment).

Taken as a whole, the results suggested that the core characteristics of HPWSs – having autonomy over task-level decision making, membership of self-directing production and offline teams, and communication with people outside the work group – generally enhance workers' levels of organizational commitment and satisfaction.

Johnny Sung and David Ashton (2005)

This survey of high-performance work practices (HPWP) was conducted in 294 UK companies. It included 10 case studies. Its aim was to study the relationship between the adoption of such practices and a range of organizational outcomes. A list of 35 HPWP practices was drawn up under the three headings of high-involvement practices, human resource practices and reward and commitment practices.

The survey provided evidence that the level of HPWP adoption as measured by the number of practices in use is linked to organizational performance. Those adopting more of the practices as 'bundles' had greater employee involvement and were more effective in delivering adequate training provision, managing staff and providing career opportunities.

Jeff Ericksen (2007)

Research was conducted in 196 small businesses to test the hypothesis that HPWSs create a human resource advantage by aligning key employee attributes and the strategic goals of the firm and by adapting their workforce attributes in response to new strategic circumstances. Dynamic workforce alignment exists when firms have 'the right types of people, in the right places, doing the right things right' and when adjustments are readily made to their workforces as the situation changes.

The research showed that there was a strong positive relationship between workforce alignment and sales growth when adaptation was high.

DEVELOPING A HIGH-PERFORMANCE STRATEGY

A high-performance strategy has to be aligned to the context of the organization and to its business strategy. Every organization will therefore develop a different strategy, as is illustrated by the case study examples set out in Table 9.2.

Approach to development

A high-performance strategy is focused on what needs to be done to reach the organization's goals. The aim is to create and maintain a high-performance culture. The approach to development is therefore based on an

Table 9.2 Examples of high-performance working ingredients

Organization	High-Performance Working Ingredients
Halo Foods	A strategy that maintains competitiveness by increasing added value through the efforts and enhanced capability of all staff.
	The integration of technical advance with people development.
	Continuing reliance on teamworking and effective leadership, with innovation and self- and team management skills.
Land Registry	Organizational changes to streamline processes, raise skill levels and release talents.
	Managers who could see that the problems were as much cultural as organizational.
	Recruitment of people whose attitudes and aptitudes match the needs of high-performance work practices.
Meritor Heavy Vehicle Braking Systems	Skill enhancement, particularly of management and self-management skills using competence frameworks.
	Teamworking skills and experience used on improvement projects.
	Linking learning, involvement and performance management.
Orangebox	A strategy that relies on constant reinvention of operational capability.
	Engagement and development of existing talent and initiative in productivity improvement.
	Increasing use of cross-departmental projects to tackle wider opportunities.
Perkinelmer	A vision and values worked through by managers and supervisors.
	Engagement of everyone in the organization and establishment of a continuous improvement culture. Learning as a basis for change.
United Welsh Housing Association	Linking of better employment relations with better performance.
	Using staff experience to improve customer service.
	Focusing management development on the cascading of a partnership culture.

Source: Stevens (2005)

understanding of what those goals are and how people can contribute to their achievement, and on assessing what type of performance culture is required as a basis for developing a high-performance work system.

The characteristics of a high-performance culture are that:

▌ a clear line of sight exists between the strategic aims of the organization and those of its departments and its staff at all levels;

▌ people know what is expected of them – they understand their goals and accountabilities;

▌ people feel that their job is worth doing, and there is a strong fit between the job and their capabilities;

█ people are empowered to maximize their contribution;

█ management defines what it requires in the shape of performance improvements, sets goals for success and monitors performance to ensure that the goals are achieved;

█ there is strong leadership from the top, which engenders a shared belief in the importance of continuing improvement;

█ there is a focus on promoting positive attitudes that result in an engaged, committed and motivated workforce;

█ performance management processes are aligned to business goals to ensure that people are engaged in achieving agreed objectives and standards;

█ capacities of people are developed through learning at all levels to support performance improvement and people are provided with opportunities to make full use of their skills and abilities;

█ a pool of talent ensures a continuous supply of high performers in key roles;

█ people are valued and rewarded according to their contribution;

█ people are involved in developing high-performance practices;

█ there is a climate of trust and teamwork, aimed at delivering a distinctive service to the customer.

High-performance work systems provide the means for creating a performance culture. They embody ways of thinking about performance in organizations and how it can be improved. They are concerned with developing and implementing bundles of complementary practices that as an integrated whole will make a much more powerful impact on performance than if they were dealt with as separate entities.

The development programme requires strong leadership from the top. Stakeholders – line managers, team leaders, employees and their representatives – should be involved as much as possible through surveys, focus groups and workshops.

Developing a high-performance work system

The steps required are described below:

1. *Analyse the business strategy:*
   - Where is the business going?
   - What are the strengths and weaknesses of the business?
   - What threats and opportunities face the business?
   - What are the implications of the above on the type of people required by the business, now and in the future?
   - To what extent does (can) the business obtain competitive advantage through people?

2. *Define the desired performance culture of the business and the objectives of the exercise.* Use the list of characteristics above as a starting point and produce a list that is aligned to the culture and context of the business and a statement of the objectives of developing an HPWS.

3. *Analyse the existing arrangements.* Start from the headings defined at stage 2 and analyse against each heading:
   - What is happening now in the form of practices, attitudes and behaviours (what do we want people to do differently)?
   - What should be happening?
   - What do people feel about it (the more involvement in this analysis from all stakeholders the better)?

4. *Identify the gaps between what is and what should be.* Clarify specific practices where there is considerable room for improvement.

5. *Draw up a list of practices that need to be introduced or improved.* At this stage only a broad definition should be produced of what ideally needs to be done.

6. *Establish complementarities.* Identify the practices that can be linked together in 'bundles' in order to complement and support one another.

7. *Assess practicality.* The ideal list of practices, or preferably bundles of practices, should be subjected to a reality check:
   - Is it worth doing? What's the business case in terms of added value? What contribution will it make to supporting the achievement of the organization's strategic goals?
   - Can it be done?
   - Who does it?
   - Have we the resources to do it?
   - How do we manage the change?

8. *Prioritize.* In the light of the assessment of practicalities, decide on the priorities that should be given to introducing new or improved practices. A realistic approach is essential. There will be a limit on how much can be done at once or any future time. Priorities should be established by assessing:
   - the added value the practice will create;
   - the availability of the resources required;
   - anticipated problems in introducing the practice, including resistance to change by stakeholders (too much should not be made of this: change can be managed, but there is much to be said for achieving some quick wins);
   - the extent to which practices can form bundles of mutually supporting practices.

9. *Define project objectives.* Develop the broad statement of objectives produced at stage 2 and define what is to be achieved, why and how.

10. *Get buy-in.* This should start at the top with the chief executive and members of the senior management team, but so far as possible it should extend to all the other stakeholders (easier if they have been involved at earlier stages and if the intentions have been fully communicated).

11. *Plan the implementation.* This is where things become difficult. Deciding what needs to be done is fairly easy; getting it done is the hard part. The implementation plan needs to cover:
    – who takes the lead: this must come from the top of the organization; nothing will work without it;
    – who manages the project and who else is involved;
    – the timetable for development and introduction;
    – the resources (people and money required);
    – how the change programme will be managed, including communication and further consultation;
    – the success criteria for the project.

12. *Implement.* Too often, 80 per cent of the time spent on introducing an HPWS is spent on planning and only 20 per cent on implementation. It should be the other way round. Whoever is responsible for implementation must have very considerable project and change management skills.

10

Corporate social responsibility strategy

Corporate social responsibility (CSR) is exercised by organizations when they conduct their business in an ethical way, taking account of the social, environmental and economic impact of how they operate and going beyond compliance. As defined by McWilliams *et al* (2006) CSR refers to the actions taken by businesses 'that further some social good beyond the interests of the firm and that which is required by law'.

CSR has also been described by Husted and Salazar (2006) as being concerned with 'the impact of business behaviour on society' and by Porter and Kramer (2006) as a process of integrating business and society. The latter argued that to advance CSR 'we must root it in a broad understanding of the interrelationship between a corporation and society while at the same time anchoring it in the strategies and activities of specific companies'.

The CIPD in *Making CSR Happen: The contribution of people management* (Redington, 2005) placed more emphasis on CSR in the workplace when it defined it as the 'continuing commitment by business to behave ethically and contribute to economic development while improving the quality of life of the workforce and their families as well as of the local community and society at large'.

STRATEGIC CSR DEFINED

Strategic CSR is about deciding initially whether or not the firm should be involved in social issues and then creating a corporate social agenda – deciding what social issues to focus on and to what extent. As Porter and Kramer (2006) emphasize, strategy is always about choice. They suggest that organizations that 'make the right choices and build focused, proactive and integrated social initiatives in concert with their core strategies will increasingly distance themselves from the pack'. They also believe that 'It is through strategic CSR that the company will make the greatest social impact and reap the greatest business benefits.' As Baron (2001) points out, CSR is what a firm does when it provides 'a public good in conjunction with its business and marketing strategy'.

CSR strategy needs to be integrated with the business strategy, but it is also closely associated with HR strategy. This is because it is concerned with ethical behaviour both outside and within the firm – with society generally and with the internal community. In the latter case this means creating a working environment where personal and employment rights are upheld and HR policies and practices provide for the fair and ethical treatment of employees.

CSR ACTIVITIES

CSR activities as listed by McWilliams *et al* (2006) include incorporating social characteristics or features into products and manufacturing processes, adopting progressive human resource management practices, achieving higher levels of environmental performance through recycling and pollution abatement and advancing the goals of community organizations.

Business in the Community (2007) surveyed the CSR activities of 120 leading British companies and summarized them under four headings:

1. *Community.* Skills and education, employability and social exclusion were frequently identified as key risks and opportunities. Other major activities were support for local community initiatives and being a responsible and safe neighbour.
2. *Environment.* Most companies reported climate change and resource use as key issues for their business, and 85 per cent of them managed their impacts through an environmental management system.
3. *Marketplace.* The issues most frequently mentioned by companies were research and development, procurement and supply chain, responsible selling, responsible marketing and product safety. There was a rising

focus on fair treatment of customers, providing appropriate product information and labelling, and the impacts of products on customer health.

4. *Workplace.* This was the strongest management performing area, as most companies have established employment management frameworks that can cater for workplace issues as they emerge. Companies recognized the crucial role of employees to achieving responsible business practices. Increasing emphasis was placed on internal communications and training to raise awareness and understanding of why it is relevant to them and valuable for the business. More attention was being paid to health and well-being issues as well as the traditional safety agenda. More work was being done on diversity, both to ensure the business attracts a diverse workforce and to communicate the business care for diversity internally.

Business in the Community also reported a growing emphasis on responsible business as a source of competitive advantage as firms move beyond minimizing risk to creating opportunities.

A survey conducted by Industrial Relations Services (Egan, 2006) found that:

▌ most employers believe that employment practices designed to ensure the fair and ethical treatment of staff can boost recruitment and retention;
▌ relatively few employers are strongly convinced of a positive link to business performance or productivity;
▌ the issue of ethics in employment is often viewed as part of a broader social responsibility package;
▌ policies on ethical employment most commonly cover HR practice in the areas of recruitment, diversity, redundancy and dismissal proceedings and employee involvement.

THE RATIONALE FOR CSR

Stakeholder theory as first propounded by Freeman (1984) suggests that managers must satisfy a variety of constituents (eg workers, customers, suppliers, local community organizations) who can influence firm outcomes. According to this view, it is not sufficient for managers to focus exclusively on the needs of stockholders or the owners of the corporation. Stakeholder theory implies that it can be beneficial for the firm to engage in certain CSR activities that non-financial stakeholders perceive to be important.

A different view was expressed by Theodore Levitt, marketing expert. In his 1958 *Harvard Business Review* article 'The dangers of social responsibility', he warned that 'government's job is not business, and business's job is not government'. Milton Friedman (1970), the Chicago monetarist, expressed the same sentiment. His maxim was that the social responsibility of business is to maximize profits within the bounds of the law. He argued that the mere existence of CSR was an agency problem within the firm in that it was a misuse of the resources entrusted to managers by owners, which could be better used on value-added internal projects or returned to the shareholders.

Generally, however, academics at least have been in favour of CSR, and there is plenty of evidence both in the UK and in the United States that many firms are pursuing CSR policies. The arguments identified by Porter and Kramer (2006) that support CSR are:

1. *The moral appeal* – the argument that companies have a duty to be good citizens. The US business association Business for Social Responsibility asks its members 'to achieve commercial success in ways that honour ethical values and respect people, communities and the natural environment'.
2. *Sustainability* – an emphasis on environmental and community stewardship. As expressed by the World Business Council for Sustainable Social Development (2006) this involves 'meeting the needs of the present without compromising the ability of future generations to meet their own needs'.
3. *Licence to operate* – every company needs tacit or explicit permission from government, communities and other stakeholders to do business.
4. *Reputation* – CSR initiatives can be justified because they improve a company's image, strengthen its brand, enliven morale and even raise the value of its stock.

The rationale for CSR as defined by Hillman and Keim (2001) is based on two propositions: first, there is a moral imperative for businesses to 'do the right thing' without regard to how such decisions affect firm performance (the social issues argument); and second, firms can achieve competitive advantage by tying CSR activities to primary stakeholders (the stakeholders argument). Their research in 500 firms implied that investing in stakeholder management may be complementary to shareholder value creation and could indeed provide a basis for competitive advantage, as important resources and capabilities are created that differentiate a firm from its competitors. However, participating in social issues beyond the direct stakeholders may adversely affect a firm's ability to create shareholder wealth.

It can be argued, as do Moran and Ghoshal (1996), 'that what is good for society does not necessarily have to be bad for the firm, and what is good for the firm does not necessarily have to come at a cost to society'. This notion may support a slightly cynical view that there is room for enlightened self-interest, which involves doing well by doing good.

Much research has been conducted on the relationship between CSR and firm performance. Russo and Fouts (1997) found that there was a positive relationship between environmental performance, and Waddock and Graves (1997) established that CSR results in an improvement in firm performance. But McWilliams and Siegel (2000) discovered only a neutral relationship between CSR and profitability.

DEVELOPING A CSR STRATEGY

The basis for developing a CSR strategy is provided by the Competency Framework of the CSR Academy (2006), which is made up of six characteristics:

1. *Understanding society* – understanding how business operates in the broader context and knowing the social and environmental impact that the business has on society.
2. *Building capacity* – building the capacity of others to help manage the business effectively. For example, suppliers understand the business's approach to the environment and employees can apply social and environmental concerns in their day-to-day roles.
3. *Questioning business-as-usual* – individuals continually questioning the business in relation to a more sustainable future and being open to improving the quality of life and the environment.
4. *Stakeholder relations* – understanding who the key stakeholders are and the risks and opportunities they present; working with them through consultation and taking their views into account.
5. *Strategic view* – ensuring that social and environmental views are included in the business strategy, for example that they are integral to the way the business operates.
6. *Harnessing diversity* – respecting that people are different, which is reflected in fair and transparent business practices.

To develop and implement a CSR strategy based on these principles it is necessary to:

▌ understand the business and social environment in which the firm operates;
▌ understand the business and HR strategies and how the CSR strategy should be aligned to them;

- know who the stakeholders are (including top management) and find out their views and expectations on CSR;
- identify the areas in which CSR activities might take place by reference to their relevance in the business context of the organization and an evaluation of their significance to stakeholders;
- prioritize as necessary on the basis of an assessment of the relevance and significance of CSR to the organization and its stakeholders and the practicalities of introducing the activity or practice;
- draw up the strategy and make the case for it to top management and the stakeholders;
- obtain approval for the CSR strategy from top management and key stakeholders;
- communicate information on the whys and wherefores of the strategy comprehensively and regularly;
- provide training to employees on the skills they need to use in implementing the CSR strategy;
- measure and evaluate the effectiveness of CSR.

11

Organization development strategy

ORGANIZATION DEVELOPMENT DEFINED

Organization development (OD) is defined by Cummins and Worley (2005) as the 'system wide application and transfer of behavioural science knowledge to the planned development, improvement and refinement of the strategies, structures and processes that lead to organizational effectiveness'. French and Bell (1990) produced the following more detailed definition:

> A planned systematic process in which applied behavioural science principles and practices are introduced into an ongoing organization towards the goals of effecting organizational improvement, greater organizational competence, and greater organizational effectiveness. The focus is on organizations and their improvement or, to put it another way, *total systems change*. The orientation is on action – achieving desired results as a result of planned activities.

Organization development aims to help people work more effectively together, improve organizational processes such as the formulation and implementation of strategy and facilitate the transformation of the organization and the management of change. As expressed by Beer (1980), OD operates as a 'system wide process of data collection, diagnosis, action planning, intervention and evaluation'.

OD is based on behavioural science concepts, but during the 1980s and 1990s the focus shifted to a number of other approaches. Some of these, such as organizational transformation, are not entirely dissimilar to OD. Others such as team building, change management and culture change or management are built on some of the basic ideas developed by writers on organization development and OD practitioners. Yet other approaches such as high-performance work systems, total quality management, business process re-engineering and performance management would be described as holistic processes that attempt to improve overall organizational effectiveness from a particular perspective. More recently, as noted by Cummins and Worley (2005), the practice of OD has gone 'far beyond its humanistic origins by incorporating concepts from organization strategy that complement the early emphasis on social processes'.

OD STRATEGIES

OD strategies concentrate on *how* things are done as well as what is done. They are concerned with system-wide change and are developed as programmes with the following features:

1. They are managed, or at least strongly supported, from the top but may make use of third parties or 'change agents' to diagnose problems and to manage change by various kinds of planned activity or 'intervention'.
2. The plans for organization development are based upon a systematic analysis and diagnosis of the strategies and circumstances of the organization and the changes and problems affecting it.
3. They use behavioural science knowledge and aim to improve the way the organization copes in times of change through such processes as interaction, communications, participation, planning and conflict management.
4. They focus on ways of ensuring that business and HR strategies are implemented and change is managed effectively.

ASSUMPTIONS AND VALUES OF OD

OD is based upon the following assumptions and values:

█ Most individuals are driven by the need for personal growth and development as long as their environment is both supportive and challenging.

▌ The work team, especially at the informal level, has great significance for feelings of satisfaction, and the dynamics of such teams have a powerful effect on the behaviour of their members.

▌ OD programmes aim to improve the quality of working life of all members of the organization.

▌ Organizations can be more effective if they learn to diagnose their own strengths and weaknesses.

▌ But managers often do not know what is wrong and need special help in diagnosing problems, although the outside 'process consultant' ensures that decision making remains in the hands of the client.

▌ The implementation of strategy involves paying close attention to the people processes involved and the management of change.

ACTIVITIES INCORPORATED IN THE OD STRATEGY

The activities that may be incorporated in an OD strategy are summarized below.

Action research

This is an approach developed by Lewin (1951) that takes the form of systematically collecting data from people about process issues and feeding the data back in order to identify problems and their likely causes. This provides the basis for an action plan to deal with the problem that can be implemented cooperatively by the people involved. The essential elements of action research are data collection, diagnosis, feedback, action planning, action and evaluation.

Survey feedback

This is a variety of action research in which data are systematically collected about the system and then fed back to groups to analyse and interpret as the basis for preparing action plans. The techniques of survey feedback include the use of attitude surveys and workshops to feed back results and discuss implications.

Interventions

The term 'intervention' in OD refers to core structured activities involving clients and consultants. The activities can take the form of action research, survey feedback or any of those mentioned below. Argyris (1970) summed up the three primary tasks of the OD practitioner or interventionist as being to:

1. generate and help clients to generate valid information that they can understand about their problems;
2. create opportunities for clients to search effectively for solutions to their problems, to make free choices;
3. create conditions for internal commitment to their choices and opportunities for the continual monitoring of the action taken.

Process consultation

As described by Schein (1969) this involves helping clients to generate and analyse information that they can understand and, following a thorough diagnosis, act upon. The information will relate to organizational processes such as inter-group relations, interpersonal relations and communications. The job of the process consultant was defined by Schein as being to 'help the organization to solve its own problems by making it aware of organizational processes, of the consequences of these processes, and of the mechanisms by which they can be changed'.

Group dynamics

Group dynamics (a term coined by Lewin, 1947) are the processes that take place in groups that determine how they act and react in different circumstances. Team-building interventions can deal with permanent work teams or those set up to deal with projects or to solve particular problems. Interventions are directed towards the analysis of the effectiveness of team processes such as problem solving, decision making and interpersonal relationships, a diagnosis and discussion of the issues, and joint consideration of the actions required to improve effectiveness.

Inter-group conflict interventions

As developed by Blake, Shepart and Mouton (1964) these aim to improve inter-group relations by getting groups to share their perceptions of one another and to analyse what they have learnt about themselves and the other group. The groups involved meet each other to share what they have learnt and to agree on the issues to be resolved and the actions required.

Personal interventions

These include sensitivity training laboratories (T-groups), transactional analysis and, more recently, neuro-linguistic programming (NLP). Another approach is behaviour modelling, which is based on Bandura's (1977) social learning theory. This states that for people to engage successfully in a behaviour they 1) must perceive a link between the behaviour and certain outcomes, 2) must desire those outcomes (this is termed 'positive valence') and 3) must believe they can do it (termed 'self-efficacy'). Behaviour modelling training involves getting a group to identify the problem and develop and practise the skills required by looking at videos or DVDs showing what skills can be applied, role-playing, practising the use of skills on the job and discussing how well they have been applied.

Integrated strategic change

Integrated strategic change methodology is a highly participative process conceived by Worley *et al* (1996). The aim is to facilitate the implementation of strategic plans. The steps required are:

1. strategic analysis, a review of the organization's strategic orientation (its strategic intentions within its competitive environment) and a diagnosis of the organization's readiness for change;
2. developing strategic capability – the ability to implement the strategic plan quickly and effectively;
3. integrating individuals and groups throughout the organization into the processes of analysis, planning and implementation to maintain the firm's strategic focus, directing attention and resources to the organization's key competencies, improving coordination and integration within the organization and creating higher levels of shared ownership and commitment;
4. creating the strategy, gaining commitment and support for it and planning its implementation;
5. implementing the strategic change plan, drawing on knowledge of motivation, group dynamics and change processes, dealing with issues such as alignment, adaptability, teamwork and organizational and individual learning;
6. allocating resources, providing feedback and solving problems as they arise.

STRATEGIES FOR ORGANIZATIONAL TRANSFORMATION

Organizational transformation is defined by Cummins and Worley (2005) as a 'process of radically altering the organization's strategic direction, including fundamental changes in structures, processes and behaviours'. Transformation involves what is called 'second-order' or 'gamma' change involving discontinuous shifts in strategy, structure, processes or culture.

Transformation is required when:

▮ significant changes occur in the competitive, technological, social or legal environment;
▮ major changes take place to the product life cycle requiring different product development and marketing strategies;
▮ major changes take place in top management;
▮ a financial crisis or large downturn occurs;
▮ an acquisition or merger takes place.

Transformation strategies

Transformation strategies are usually driven by senior management and line managers with the support of HR rather than OD specialists. The key roles of management as defined by Tushman *et al* (1988) are envisioning, energizing and enabling.

Organizational transformation strategic plans may involve radical changes to the structure, culture and processes of the organization – the way it looks at the world. They may involve planning and implementing significant and far-reaching developments in corporate structures and organization-wide processes. The change is neither incremental (bit by bit) nor transactional (concerned solely with systems and procedures). Transactional change, according to Pascale (1990), is merely concerned with the alteration of ways in which the organization does business and people interact with one another on a day-to-day basis and 'is effective when what you want is more of what you've already got'. He advocates a 'discontinuous improvement in capability', and this he describes as transformation.

Types of transformational strategies

Four strategies for transformational change have been identified by Beckhard (1989):

1. *a change in what drives the organization*, for example a change from being production-driven to being market-driven would be transformational;
2. *a fundamental change in the relationships between or among organizational parts*, for example decentralization;
3. *a major change in the ways of doing work*, for example the introduction of new technology such as computer-integrated manufacturing;
4. *a basic, cultural change in norms, values or research systems*, for example developing a customer-focused culture.

Transformation through leadership

Transformation programmes are led from the top within the organization. They do not rely on an external 'change agent' as did traditional OD interventions, although specialist external advice might be obtained on aspects of the transformation such as strategic planning, reorganization or developing new reward processes.

The prerequisite for a successful programme is the presence of a transformational leader who, as defined by Burns (1978), motivates others to strive for higher-order goals rather than merely short-term interest. Transformational leaders go beyond dealing with day-to-day management problems; they commit people to action and focus on the development of new levels of awareness of where the future lies, and commitment to achieving that future. Burns contrasts transformational leaders with transactional leaders, who operate by building up a network of interpersonal transactions in a stable situation and who enlist compliance rather than commitment through the reward system and the exercise of authority and power. Transactional leaders may be good at dealing with here-and-now problems but they will not provide the vision required to transform the future.

Managing the transition

Strategies need to be developed for managing the transition from where the organization is to where the organization wants to be. This is the critical part of a transformation programme. It is during the transition period of getting from here to there that change takes place. Transition management starts from a definition of the future state and a diagnosis of the present state. It is then necessary to define what has to be done to achieve the transformation. This means deciding on the new processes, systems, procedures, structures, products and markets to be developed. Having defined these, the work can be programmed and the resources required (people, money, equipment and time) can be defined. The strategic plan for managing the transition should include provisions for involving people in the process and for communicating to them about what is happening, why it is happening and how it will affect them. Clearly the aims are to get as many people as possible committed to the change.

The transformation programme

The eight steps required to transform an organization have been summed up by Kotter (1995) as follows:

1. *Establishing a sense of urgency:*
   - examining market and competitive realities;

    – identifying and discussing crises, potential crises or major opportunities.

2. *Forming a powerful guiding coalition:*
   - assembling a group with enough power to lead the change effort;
   - encouraging the group to work together as a team.

3. *Creating a vision:*
   - creating a vision to help direct the change effort;
   - developing strategies for achieving that vision.

4. *Communicating the vision:*
   - using every vehicle possible to communicate the new vision and strategies;
   - teaching new behaviours by the example of the guiding coalition.

5. *Empowering others to act on the vision:*
   - getting rid of obstacles to change;
   - changing systems or structures that seriously undermine the vision;
   - encouraging risk taking and non-traditional ideas, activities and actions.

6. *Planning for and creating short-term wins:*
   - planning for visible performance improvement;
   - creating those improvements;
   - recognizing and rewarding employees involved in the improvements.

7. *Consolidating improvements and producing still more change:*
   - using increased credibility to change systems, structures and policies that don't fit the vision;
   - hiring, promoting and developing employees who can implement the vision;
   - reinvigorating the process with new projects, themes and change agents.

8. *Institutionalizing new approaches:*
   - articulating the connections between the new behaviours and corporate success;
   - developing the means to ensure leadership development and succession.

Transformation capability

The development and implementation of transformation strategies require special capabilities. As Gratton (1999) points out: 'Transformation capability depends in part on the ability to create and embed processes which link business strategy to the behaviours and performance of individuals and teams. These clusters of processes link vertically (to create alignment with short-term business needs), horizontally (to create cohesion), and temporally (to transform to meet future business needs).'

12

Employee engagement strategy

Engaged people at work are positive, interested in and even excited about their jobs and prepared to go the extra mile to get them done to the best of their ability. As defined by Towers Perrin (2007), the term employee engagement refers to 'the extent to which employees put discretionary effort into their work, beyond the minimum to get the job done, in the form of extra time, brainpower or energy'. An engagement strategy will address all the means that an organization can use to promote this type of effort.

This chapter starts with a discussion of the difference between employee engagement and organizational commitment, two concepts that are frequently confused. The chapter continues with sections on the significance of engagement, engagement and discretionary behaviour, what constitutes an engaged employee, the factors that influence engagement, strategies for enhancing engagement, and measuring engagement.

ENGAGEMENT AND ORGANIZATIONAL COMMITMENT

Engagement and organizational commitment are two important concepts affecting work performance and the attraction and retention of employees. However, the two concepts are often confused. For example, the Conference

Board in the United States (2006) defines engagement as 'a heightened connection that an employee feels for his or her organization'.

They are indeed closely linked – high organizational commitment can increase engagement and high engagement can increase commitment. But people can be engaged with their work even when they are not committed to the organization except in so far as it gives them the opportunity to use and develop their skills. This may be the case with some knowledge workers. For example, researchers may be mainly interested in the facilities for research they are given and the opportunity to make a name for themselves. They therefore join and stay with an organization only if it gives them the opportunities they seek. Combinations of engagement and organizational commitment are illustrated in Figure 12.1.

THE SIGNIFICANCE OF ENGAGEMENT

The significance of engagement is that it is at the heart of the employment relationship. It is about what people do and how they behave in their roles and what makes them act in ways that further the achievement of the objectives of both the organization and themselves. Research reported by Watkin (2002) found that there were significant differences in value-added discretionary performance between 'superior' and 'standard' performers. The difference in low-complexity jobs was 19 per cent, in moderate-complexity jobs 32 per cent and in high-complexity jobs 48 per cent.

Figure 12.1 Combinations of the impact of engagement and organizational commitment

ENGAGEMENT AND DISCRETIONARY BEHAVIOUR

There is a close link between high levels of engagement and positive discretionary behaviour. As described by Purcell *et al* (2003) discretionary behaviour refers to the choices that people at work often have on the way they do the job and the amount of effort, care, innovation and productive behaviour they display. It can be positive when people 'go the extra mile' to achieve high levels of performance. It can be negative when they exercise their discretion to slack at their work. Discretionary behaviour is hard for the employer to define and monitor, and the amount of discretionary behaviour required is hard for the employer to control. But positive discretionary behaviour is more likely to happen when people are engaged with their work.

The propositions made by Purcell *et al* on discretionary behaviour as a result of their longitudinal research in association with the Chartered Institute of Personnel and Development (CIPD) were that:

▌ performance-related practices only work if they positively induce discretionary behaviour, once basic staffing requirements have been met;

▌ discretionary behaviour is more likely to occur when enough individuals have commitment to their organization and/or when they feel motivated to do so and/or when they gain high levels of job satisfaction;

▌ commitment, motivation and job satisfaction, either together or separately, will be higher when people positively experience the application of HR policies concerned with creating an able workforce, motivating valued behaviours and providing opportunities to participate;

▌ this positive experience will be higher if the wide range of HR policies necessary to develop ability, motivation and opportunity both are in place and are mutually reinforcing;

▌ the way HR and reward policies and practices are implemented by front-line managers and the way top-level espoused values and organizational cultures are enacted by them will enhance or weaken the effect of HR policies in triggering discretionary behaviour by influencing attitudes;

▌ the experience of success seen in performance outcomes helps reinforce positive attitudes.

WHAT IS AN ENGAGED EMPLOYEE?

An answer to this question was provided by Bevan, Barber and Robinson (1997), who describe an engaged employee as someone 'who is aware of business context, and works closely with colleagues to improve performance within the job for the benefit of the organization'.

A more detailed answer was given by Robinson *et al* (2004), whose research for the Institute of Employment Studies indicated that an engaged employee was someone who:

█ is positive about the job;
█ believes in, and identifies with, the organization;
█ works actively to make things better;
█ treats others with respect, and helps colleagues to perform more effectively;
█ can be relied upon, and goes beyond the requirements of the job;
█ sees the bigger picture, even sometimes at personal cost;
█ keeps up to date with developments in his or her field;
█ looks for, and is given, opportunities to improve organizational performance.

WHAT ARE THE FACTORS THAT INFLUENCE ENGAGEMENT?

Research cited by Incomes Data Services (IDS) (2007) has identified two key elements that have to be present if genuine engagement is to exist. The first is the rational aspect, which relates to employees' understanding of their role, where it fits in the wider organization and how it aligns with business objectives. The second is the emotional aspect, which has to do with how people feel about the organization, whether their work gives them a sense of personal accomplishment and how they relate to their manager.

These two overall aspects can be analysed into a number of factors that influence levels of engagement as set out below.

The work itself

The work itself can create job satisfaction leading to intrinsic motivation and increased engagement. The factors involved are interesting and challenging work, responsibility (feeling that the work is important and having control over one's own resources), autonomy (freedom to act), scope to use and develop skills and abilities, the availability of the resources required to carry out the work, and opportunities for advancement.

The work environment

An enabling, supportive and inspirational work environment creates experiences that impact on engagement by influencing how people regard their roles and carry them out. An enabling environment will create the conditions that encourage high-performance and effective discretionary behaviour. These include work processes, equipment and facilities, and the physical conditions in which people work. A supportive environment will be one in which proper attention is paid to achieving a satisfactory work–life balance, emotional demands are not excessive, attention is paid to providing healthy and safe working conditions, job security is a major consideration and personal growth needs are taken into consideration. An inspirational environment will be where what John Purcell and his colleagues refer to as 'the big idea' is present – the organization has a clear vision and a set of integrated values that are 'embedded, collective, measured and managed'.

The environment is affected by the organization's climate, which, as defined by French *et al* (1985), is 'the relatively persistent set of perceptions held by organization members concerning the characteristics and quality of organizational culture'. It is also directly influenced by its work and HR practices. As Purcell (2001) points out, the way HR practices are experienced by employees is affected by organizational values and operational strategies, such as staffing policies or hours of work, as well as the way they are implemented. He also emphasizes that work climate (how people get on in the organization) and the experience of actually doing the job (pace, demand and stress) all influence the way employees experience the work environment. This has an important effect on how they react to HR and reward practices and how these influence organizational outcomes. Employees react in a number of different ways to practices in their organization, and this affects the extent to which they want to learn more and are committed and satisfied with their jobs. This, in turn, influences engagement – how well they do their jobs and whether they are prepared to contribute discretionary effort.

Leadership

The degree to which jobs encourage engagement and positive discretionary behaviour very much depends upon the ways in which job holders are led and managed. Managers and team leaders often have considerable discretion on how jobs are designed, how they allocate work and how much they delegate and provide autonomy. They can spell out the significance of the work people do. They can give them the opportunity to achieve and develop, and provide feedback that recognizes their contribution.

Opportunities for personal growth

Most people want to get on. As Ed Lawler put it in 2003, 'People enjoy learning – there's no doubt about it – and it touches on an important "treat people right" principle for both organizations and people: the value of continuous, ongoing training and development.' Learning is a satisfying and rewarding experience and makes a significant contribution to intrinsic motivation. Alderfer (1972) emphasized the importance of the chance to grow as a means of rewarding people. He wrote: 'Satisfaction of growth needs depends on a person finding the opportunity to be what he or she is most fully and become what he or she can.' The opportunity to grow and develop is a motivating factor that directly impacts on engagement when it is an intrinsic element of the work.

Opportunities to contribute

Engagement is enhanced if employees have a voice that is listened to. This enables them to feed their ideas and views upwards and feel that they are making a contribution.

STRATEGIES FOR ENHANCING ENGAGEMENT

Engagement strategies can be developed under the headings of the factors affecting engagement set out above.

The work itself

Intrinsic motivation through the work itself, and therefore engagement, depends basically on the way in which work or jobs are designed. Three characteristics have been distinguished by Lawler (1969) as being required in jobs if they are to be intrinsically motivating:

▌ *Feedback* – individuals must receive meaningful feedback about their performance, preferably by evaluating their own performance and defining the feedback. This implies that they should ideally work on a complete product, process or service, or a significant part of it that can be seen as a whole.
▌ *Use of abilities* – the job must be perceived by individuals as requiring them to use abilities they value in order to perform the job effectively.
▌ *Self-control (autonomy)* – individuals must feel that they have a high degree of self-control over setting their own goals and over defining the paths to these goals.

These approaches may be used when setting up new work systems or jobs, and the strategy should include provision for guidance and advice along these lines to those responsible for such developments. But the greatest impact on the levels of engagement arising from the design of work systems or jobs is made by line managers on a day-to-day basis. The strategy should therefore include arrangements for educating them as part of a leadership development programme in the importance of good work and job design, the part they can play and the benefits to them arising from thereby enhancing engagement. Performance management, with its emphasis on agreeing role expectations, is a useful means of doing this.

The work environment

A strategy for increasing engagement through the work environment will be generally concerned with developing a culture that encourages positive attitudes to work, promoting interest and excitement in the jobs people do and reducing stress. Lands' End believes that staff who are enjoying themselves, who are being supported and developed and who feel fulfilled and respected at work will provide the best service to customers. The thinking behind why the company wants to inspire staff is straightforward – employees' willingness to do that little bit extra arises from their sense of pride in what the organization stands for, ie quality, service and value. It makes the difference between a good experience for customers and a poor one.

The strategy also needs to consider particular aspects of the work environment, especially communications, involvement, work–life balance and working conditions. It can include the formulation and application of 'talent relationship management' policies, which are concerned with building effective relationships with people in their roles, treating individual employees fairly, recognizing their value, giving them a voice and providing opportunities for growth.

Leadership

The leadership strategy should concentrate on what line managers have to do as leaders in order to play their vital and immediate part in increasing levels of engagement. This will include the implementation of learning programmes that help them to understand how they are expected to act and the skills they need to use. The programmes can include formal training (especially for potential managers or those in their first leadership role), but more impact will be made by 'blending' various learning methods such as e-learning, coaching and mentoring.

It should also be recognized that a performance management process can provide line managers with a useful framework in which they can deploy their skills in improving performance though increased engagement. This applies particularly to the performance management activities of role definition, performance improvement planning, joint involvement in monitoring performance, and feedback. The strategy should therefore include the steps required to make performance management more effective by increasing the commitment of managers to it and developing the skills they require.

Opportunities for personal growth

A strategy for providing development and growth opportunities should be based on the creation of a learning culture. This is one that promotes learning because it is recognized by top management, line managers and employees generally as an essential organizational process to which they are committed and in which they engage continuously. Reynolds (2004) describes a learning culture as a 'growth medium' that will 'encourage employees to commit to a range of positive discretionary behaviours, including learning', and that has the following characteristics: empowerment not supervision, self-managed learning not instruction, and long-term capacity building not short-term fixes. It will encourage discretionary learning, which Sloman (2003) believes takes place when individuals actively seek to acquire the knowledge and skills that promote the organization's objectives.

Specifically, the strategy should define the steps required to ensure that people have the opportunity and are given the encouragement to learn and grow in their roles. This includes the use of policies that focus on role flexibility – giving people the chance to develop their roles by making better and extended use of their talents. This means going beyond talent management for the favoured few and developing the abilities of the core people on whom the organization depends. The philosophy should be that everyone has the ability to succeed, and the aim should be to 'achieve extraordinary results with ordinary people'. It includes using performance management primarily as a developmental process with an emphasis on personal development planning.

The strategy should also cover career development opportunities and how individuals can be given the guidance, support and encouragement they need if they are to fulfil their potential and achieve a successful career with the organization in tune with their talents and aspirations. The actions required to provide men and women of promise with a sequence of learning activities and experiences that will equip them for whatever level of responsibility they have the ability to reach should be included in the strategy.

Opportunities to contribute

Providing people with the opportunity to contribute is not just a matter of setting up formal consultative processes, although they can be important. It is also about creating a work environment that gives people a voice by encouraging them to have their say, and emphasizes as a core value of the organization that management at all levels must be prepared to listen and respond to any contributions their people make.

MEASURING ENGAGEMENT

When developing engagement strategies the first step is to establish what is happening now and in the light of that determine what should happen in each of the areas described above. This means measuring levels of engagement regularly in order to identify successes and failures and analyse any gaps between what is wanted and what is actually going on. This can be done through published surveys such as those operated by Gallup, which enable benchmarking to take place with the levels of engagement achieved in other organizations. Alternatively organizations can develop their own surveys to suit their circumstances. An example of such a survey is provided in the SHRM toolkit in Part 4 of this book.

13

Knowledge management strategy

Knowledge management strategies aim to capture an organization's collective expertise and distribute it to 'wherever it can achieve the biggest payoff' (Blake, 1988). This is in accordance with the resource-based view of the firm, which, as argued by Grant (1991), suggests that the source of competitive advantage lies within the firm (ie in its people and their knowledge), not in how it positions itself in the market. Trussler (1998) comments that 'the capability to gather, lever, and use knowledge effectively will become a major source of competitive advantage in many businesses over the next few years'. A successful company is a knowledge-creating company.

THE PROCESS OF KNOWLEDGE MANAGEMENT

Knowledge management is 'any process or practice of creating, acquiring, capturing, sharing and using knowledge, wherever it resides, to enhance learning and performance in organizations' (Scarborough *et al* 1999). They suggest that it focuses on the development of firm-specific knowledge and skills that are the result of organizational learning processes. Knowledge management is concerned with both stocks and flows of knowledge. Stocks included expertise and encoded knowledge in computer systems. Flows represent the ways in which knowledge is transferred from people to people or from people to a knowledge database.

The purpose of knowledge management is to transfer knowledge from those who have it to those who need it in order to improve organizational effectiveness. It is concerned with storing and sharing the wisdom and understanding accumulated in an organization about its processes, techniques and operations. It treats knowledge as a key resource. It can be argued that, in the information age, knowledge rather than physical assets or financial resources is the key to competitiveness. In essence, as pointed out by Mecklenberg *et al* (1999), 'Knowledge management allows companies to capture, apply and generate value from their employees' creativity and expertise.'

Knowledge management is as much if not more concerned with people and how they acquire, exchange and disseminate knowledge as it is about information technology. That is why it has become an important strategic HRM area. Scarborough *et al* (1999) believe that HR specialists should have 'the ability to analyse the different types of knowledge deployed by the organization... [and] to relate such knowledge to issues of organizational design, career patterns and employment security'.

The concept of knowledge management is closely associated with intellectual capital theory in that it refers to the notions of human, social and organizational or structural capital. It is also linked to the concepts of organizational learning and the learning organization as discussed in Chapter 16.

Knowledge management involves transforming knowledge resources by identifying relevant information and then disseminating it so that learning can take place. Knowledge management strategies promote the sharing of knowledge by linking people with people and by linking them to information so that they learn from documented experiences.

SOURCES AND TYPES OF KNOWLEDGE

Strategies for knowledge management should be founded on an understanding of the sources and types of knowledge to be found in organizations.

Knowledge can be stored in databanks and found in presentations, reports, libraries, policy documents and manuals. It can be moved around the organization through information systems and by traditional methods such as meetings, workshops, courses, 'master classes', written publications, videos, DVDs and tapes. The intranet provides an additional and very effective medium for communicating knowledge.

As argued by Nonaka (1991) and Nonaka and Takeuchi (1995), knowledge is either explicit or tacit. Explicit knowledge can be codified – it is recorded and available and is held in databases, corporate intranets and intellectual property portfolios. Tacit knowledge exists in people's minds. It is difficult to articulate in writing and is acquired through personal experience. Hansen *et al* (1999) suggest that it includes scientific or technological expertise, operational know-how, insights about an industry, and business judgement. The main challenge in knowledge management is how to turn tacit knowledge into explicit knowledge.

APPROACHES TO THE DEVELOPMENT OF KNOWLEDGE MANAGEMENT STRATEGIES

Two approaches to knowledge management have been identified by Hansen *et al* (1999).

The first is the *codification strategy* – knowledge is carefully codified and stored in databases where it can be accessed and used easily by anyone in the organization. Knowledge is explicit and is codified using a 'people-to-document' approach. This strategy is therefore document-driven. Knowledge is extracted from the person who developed it, made independent of that person and reused for various purposes. It will be stored in some form of electronic repository for people to use, which allows many people to search for and retrieve codified knowledge without having to contact the person who originally developed it. This strategy relies largely on information technology to manage databases and also on the use of the intranet.

The second is the *personalization strategy* – knowledge is closely tied to the person who has developed it and is shared mainly through direct person-to-person contacts. This is a 'person-to-person' approach, which involves sharing tacit knowledge. The exchange is achieved by creating networks and encouraging face-to-face communication between individuals and teams by means of informal conferences, communities of practice, workshops, brainstorming and one-to-one sessions.

The research conducted by Hansen *et al* established that companies that use knowledge effectively pursue one strategy predominantly and use the second strategy to support the first. Those that try to excel at both strategies risk failing at both.

STRATEGIC KNOWLEDGE MANAGEMENT ISSUES

The following need to be addressed in developing knowledge management processes.

The pace of change

How can the strategy ensure that knowledge management processes keep up with the pace of change and identify what knowledge needs to be captured and shared?

Relating knowledge management strategy to business strategy

Hansen, *et al* (1999) assert that it is not knowledge per se but the way it is applied to strategic objectives that is the critical ingredient in competitiveness. They point out that 'competitive strategy must drive knowledge management strategy' and that managements have to answer the question 'How does knowledge that resides in the company add value for customers?' Mecklenberg *et al* (1999) argue that organizations should 'start with the business value of what they gather. If it doesn't generate value, drop it.'

Technology and people

Technology is central to organizations adopting a codification strategy. But, for those following a broader and potentially more productive personalization strategy, IT assumes more of a supportive role. As Hansen *et al* (1999) comment, 'In the codification model, managers need to implement a system that is much like a traditional library – it must contain a large cache of documents and include search engines that allow people to find and use the documents they need. In the personalization model, it's more important to have a system that allows people to find other people.'

Scarborough *et al* (1999) suggest that 'technology should be viewed more as a means of communication and less as a means of storing knowledge'. Knowledge management is more about people than technology. As research by Davenport (1996) established, managers get two-thirds of their information from face-to-face or telephone conversations. There is a limit to how much tacit knowledge can be codified. In organizations relying more on tacit than explicit knowledge, a person-to-person approach works best, and IT can only support this process; it cannot replace it.

The significance of process and social capital and culture

A preoccupation with technology may mean that too little attention is paid to the processes (social, technological and organizational) through which knowledge combines and interacts in different ways (Blackler, 1995). The key process is the interactions between people. This constitutes the social capital of an organization, ie the 'network of relationships [that] constitute a valuable resource for the conduct of social affairs' (Nahapiet and Ghoshal, 1998). Social networks can be particularly important to ensure that knowledge is shared. What is also required is another aspect of social capital, ie trust. People will not be willing to share knowledge with those whom they do not trust.

The culture of the company may inhibit knowledge sharing. The norm may be for people to keep knowledge to themselves as much as they can because 'knowledge is power'. An open culture will encourage people to share their ideas and knowledge.

COMPONENTS OF A KNOWLEDGE MANAGEMENT STRATEGY

A knowledge management strategy could be concerned with organizational people management processes that help to develop an open culture in which the values and norms emphasize the importance of sharing knowledge and facilitate knowledge sharing through networks. It might aim to encourage the development of communities of practice (defined by Wenger and Snyder, 2000, as 'groups of people informally bound together by shared expertise and a passion for joint enterprise'). The strategy could refer to methods of motivating people to share knowledge and rewarding those who do so. The development of processes of organizational and individual learning including the use of seminars and symposia that will generate and assist in disseminating knowledge could also be part of the strategy.

14

Employee resourcing strategy

Employee resourcing strategy is concerned with ensuring that the organization obtains and retains the people it needs and employs them efficiently. It is a key part of the strategic human resource management process, which is fundamentally about matching human resources to the strategic and operational needs of the organization and ensuring the full utilization of those resources. It is concerned not only with obtaining and keeping the number and quality of staff required but also with selecting and promoting people who 'fit' the culture and the strategic requirements of the organization.

THE OBJECTIVE OF EMPLOYEE RESOURCING STRATEGY

The objective of employee resourcing strategy as expressed by Keep (1989) is 'To obtain the right basic material in the form of a workforce endowed with the appropriate qualities, skills, knowledge and potential for future training. The selection and recruitment of workers best suited to meeting the needs of the organization ought to form a core activity upon which most other HRM policies geared towards development and motivation could be built.'

The concept that the strategic capability of a firm depends on its resource capability in the shape of people (the resource-based view) provides the rationale for resourcing strategy. The aim of this strategy is therefore to ensure that a firm achieves competitive advantage by employing more capable people than its rivals. These people will have a wider and deeper range of skills and will behave in ways that will maximize their contribution. The organization attracts such people by being 'the employer of choice'. It retains them by providing better opportunities and rewards than others and by developing a positive psychological contract that increases commitment and creates mutual trust. Furthermore, the organization deploys its people in ways that maximize the added value they supply.

THE STRATEGIC HRM APPROACH TO RESOURCING

HRM places more emphasis than traditional personnel management on finding people whose attitudes and behaviour are likely to be congruent with what management believes to be appropriate and conducive to success. In the words of Townley (1989), organizations are concentrating more on 'the attitudinal and behavioural characteristics of employees'. This tendency has its dangers. Innovative and adaptive organizations need non-conformists, even mavericks, who can 'buck the system'. If managers recruit people 'in their own image' there is the risk of staffing the organization with conformist clones and of perpetuating a dysfunctional culture – one that may have been successful in the past but is no longer appropriate in the face of new challenges (as Pascale, 1990, puts it, 'nothing fails like success').

The HRM approach to resourcing therefore emphasizes that matching resources to organizational requirements does not simply mean maintaining the status quo and perpetuating a moribund culture. It can and often does mean radical changes in thinking about the skills and behaviours required in the future to achieve sustainable growth and cultural change.

INTEGRATING BUSINESS AND RESOURCING STRATEGIES

The philosophy behind the strategic HRM approach to resourcing is that it is people who implement the strategic plan. As Quinn Mills (1983) has put it, the process is one of 'planning with people in mind'.

The integration of business and resourcing strategies is based on an understanding of the direction in which the organization is going and the determination of:

▌ the numbers of people required to meet business needs;
▌ the skills and behaviour required to support the achievement of business strategies;
▌ the impact of organizational restructuring as a result of rationalization, decentralization, delayering, acquisitions, mergers, product or market

development, or the introduction of new technology, for example cellular manufacturing;

▮ plans for changing the culture of the organization in such areas as ability to deliver, performance standards, quality, customer service, team-working and flexibility, which indicate the need for people with different attitudes, beliefs and personal characteristics.

These factors will be strongly influenced by the type of business strategies adopted by the organization and the sort of business it is in. These may be expressed in such terms as the Boston Consulting Group's classification of businesses as wild cat, star, cash cow or dog, or Miles and Snow's (1978) typology of defender, prospector and analyser organizations.

Resourcing strategies exist to provide the people and skills required to support the business strategy, but they should also contribute to the formulation of that strategy. HR directors have an obligation to point out to their colleagues the human resource opportunities and constraints that will affect the achievement of strategic plans. In mergers or acquisitions, for example, the ability of management within the company to handle the new situation and the quality of management in the new business will be important considerations.

BUNDLING RESOURCING STRATEGIES AND ACTIVITIES

Employee resourcing is not just about recruitment and selection. It is concerned with any means available to meet the needs of the firm for certain skills and behaviours. A strategy to enlarge the skill base may start with recruitment and selection but would also extend into learning and development to enhance skills and modify behaviours, and methods of rewarding people for the acquisition of extra skills. Performance management processes can be used to identify development needs (skill and behavioural) and motivate people to make the most effective use of their skills. Competence frameworks and profiles can be prepared to define the skills and behaviours required and used in selection, employee development and employee reward processes. The aim should be to develop a reinforcing bundle of strategies along these lines. Talent management is a 'bundling' process, which is an aspect of resourcing.

THE COMPONENTS OF EMPLOYEE RESOURCING STRATEGY

The components of employee resourcing strategy as considered here are:

▨ *Human resource planning (often referred to, especially in the public sector, as workforce planning)* – assessing future business needs and deciding on the numbers and types of people required.

▨ *Developing the organization's employee value proposition and its employer brand.*

▨ *Resourcing plans* – preparing plans for finding people from within the organization and/or for learning and development programmes to help people learn new skills. If needs cannot be satisfied from within the organization, it involves preparing longer-term plans for ensuring that recruitment and selection processes will satisfy them.

▨ *Retention strategy* – preparing plans for retaining the people the organization needs.

▨ *Flexibility strategy* – planning for increased flexibility in the use of human resources to enable the organization to make the best use of people and adapt swiftly to changing circumstances.

▨ *Talent management strategy* – ensuring that the organization has the talented people it requires to provide for management succession and meet present and future business needs (see Chapter 15).

HUMAN RESOURCE PLANNING

Defined

Human resource or workforce planning determines the human resources required by the organization to achieve its strategic goals. As defined by Bulla and Scott (1994) it is 'the process for ensuring that the human resource requirements of an organization are identified and plans are made for satisfying those requirements'. Human resource planning is based on the belief that people are an organization's most important strategic resource. It is generally concerned with matching resources to business needs in the longer term, although it will sometimes address shorter-term requirements. It addresses human resource needs both in quantitative and in qualitative terms. This means answering two basic questions: 1) how many people? and 2) what sort of people? Human resource planning also looks at broader issues relating to the ways in which people are employed and developed in order to improve organizational effectiveness. It can therefore play an important part in strategic human resource management.

Link to business planning

Human resource planning should be an integral part of business planning. The strategic planning process defines projected changes in the types of activities carried out by the organization and the scale of those activities. It identifies the core competences the organization needs to achieve its goals and therefore its skill and behavioural requirements.

Human resource planning interprets these plans in terms of people requirements. But it may influence the business strategy by drawing attention to ways in which people could be developed and deployed more effectively to further the achievement of business goals as well as focusing on any problems that might have to be resolved in order to ensure that the people required will be available and will be capable of making the necessary contribution. As Quinn Mills (1983) indicates, human resource planning is 'a decision-making process that combines three important activities: (1) identifying and acquiring the right number of people with the proper skills, (2) motivating them to achieve high performance, and (3) creating interactive links between business objectives and people-planning activities'.

Hard and soft human resource planning

A distinction can be made between 'hard' and 'soft' human resource planning. The former is based on quantitative analysis in order to ensure that the right number of the right sort of people are available when needed. The latter, as described by Marchington and Wilkinson (1996), 'is more explicitly focused on creating and shaping the culture of the organization so that there is a clear integration between corporate goals and employee values, beliefs and behaviours'. But, as they point out, the soft version becomes virtually synonymous with the whole subject of human resource management.

Human resource planning is indeed concerned with broader issues about the employment of people than the traditional quantitative approach of 'manpower planning'. But it also addresses those aspects of human resource management that are primarily about the organization's requirements for people from the viewpoint of numbers, skills and how they are deployed. This is the sense in which human resource planning is discussed in this chapter.

Limitations

However, it must be recognized that although the notion of human resource planning is well established in the HRM vocabulary it does not seem to be embedded as a key HR activity. As Rothwell (1995) suggests, 'Apart from isolated examples, there has been little research evidence of increased use or of its success.' She explains the gap between theory and practice as arising from:

▌ the impact of change and the difficulty of predicting the future – 'the need for planning may be in inverse proportion to its feasibility';

▌ the 'shifting kaleidoscope' of policy priorities and strategies within organizations;

▌ the distrust displayed by many managers of theory or planning – they often prefer pragmatic adaptation to conceptualization;

▌ the lack of evidence that human resource planning works.

Research conducted by Cowling and Walters (1990) indicated that the only formal and regular activities carried out by respondents were the identification of future training needs, analysis of training costs and analysis of productivity. Less than half produced formal labour supply and demand forecasts, and less than 20 per cent formally monitored HR planning practices.

Summarizing the problem, Taylor (1998) comments that 'It would seem that employers, quite simply, prefer to wait until their view of the future environment clears sufficiently for them to see the whole picture before committing resources in preparation for its arrival. The perception is that the more complex and turbulent the environment, the more important it is to wait and see before acting.'

Be that as it may, it is difficult to reject out of hand the belief that some attempt should be made broadly to determine future human resource requirements as a basis for strategic planning and action.

Approaches to human resource planning

Resourcing strategies show the way forward through the analysis of business strategies and demographic trends. They are converted into action plans based on the outcome of the following interrelated planning activities:

▌ *Demand forecasting* – estimate future needs for people and competences by reference to corporate and functional plans and forecasts of future activity levels.

▌ *Supply forecasting* – estimate the supply of people by reference to analyses of current resources and future availability, after allowing for wastage. The forecast will also take account of labour market trends relating to the availability of skills and to demographics.

▌ *Forecasting requirements* – analyse the demand and supply forecasts to identify future deficits or surpluses, with the help of models where appropriate.

▌ *Action planning* – prepare plans to deal with forecast deficits through internal promotion, training or external recruitment. If necessary, plan for unavoidable downsizing so as to avoid any compulsory redundancies, if that is possible. Develop retention and flexibility strategies.

Although these are described as separate areas they are closely interrelated and often overlap. For example, demand forecasts are estimates of future requirements, and these may be prepared on the basis of assumptions about the productivity of employees. But the supply forecast will also have to consider productivity trends and how they might affect the supply of people.

A flow chart of the process of human resource planning is shown in Figure 14.1.

EMPLOYEE VALUE PROPOSITION

An organization's employee value proposition consists of what it has to offer prospective or existing employees if they join or remain with the business. It will include remuneration – which is important but can be overemphasized

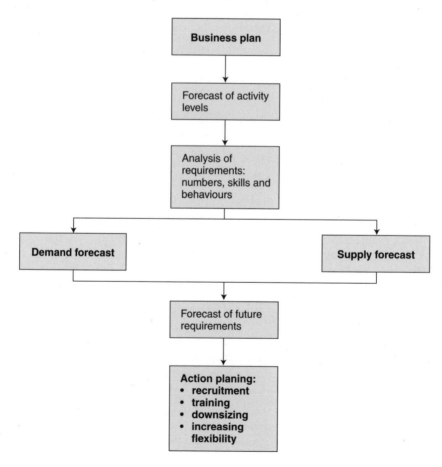

Figure 14.1 Human resource planning flow chart

compared with other elements. These non-financial factors may be crucial in attracting and retaining people and include:

- the attractiveness of the organization;
- responsibility – corporate conduct and ethics;
- respect – diversity and inclusion;
- work–life balance;
- opportunities for personal and professional growth.

The employee value proposition can be expressed as an employer brand, defined by Walker (2007) as 'a set of attributes and qualities – often intangible – that make an organization distinctive, promise a particular kind of employment experience and appeal to people who will thrive and perform their best in its culture'. Employer branding is the creation of a brand image of the organization for prospective employees. It will be influenced by the reputation of the organization as a business or provider of services as well as its reputation as an employer. To create an employer brand it is necessary to:

- analyse what ideal candidates need and want and take this into account in deciding what should be offered and how it should be offered;
- establish how far the core values of the organization support the creation of an attractive brand and ensure that these are incorporated in the presentation of the brand as long as they are 'values in use' (lived by members of the organization) rather than simply espoused;
- define the features of the brand on the basis of an examination and review of each of the areas that affect the perceptions of people about the organization as 'a great place to work' – the way people are treated, the provision of a fair deal, opportunities for growth, work–life balance, leadership, the quality of management, involvement with colleagues and how and why the organization is successful;
- benchmark the approaches of other organizations (the *Sunday Times* list of the 100 best companies to work for is useful) to obtain ideas about what can be done to enhance the brand;
- be honest and realistic.

RESOURCING PLANS

The analysis of future requirements should indicate what steps need to be taken to appoint people from within the organization and what training programmes should be planned. The analysis will also establish how many people will need to be recruited in the absence of qualified employees within the organization or the impossibility of training people in the new skills in time.

Internal resourcing

Ideally, internal resourcing should be based on data already available about skills and potential. This should have been provided by regular skills audits and the analysis of the outcomes of performance management reviews. A 'trawl' can then be made to locate available talent, which can be accompanied by an internal advertising campaign.

External resourcing

External resourcing requirements can be met by developing a recruitment strategy. The aims of this strategy should be first to make the organization 'the employer of choice' in its particular field or for the people it wants to recruit (eg graduates). Second, the strategy should plan the best methods of defining precisely what is needed in terms of skills and competencies. Finally, the strategy should be concerned with planning the use of the most effective methods of obtaining the number and type of people required. As indicated by Spellman (1992) the strategy should be developed as follows:

1. *Define skill and competency (behavioural) requirements.* Ideally this should be carried out by the use of systematic skill and competency analysis techniques. These can form the material upon which focused and structured interviews can take place and be used as criteria for selection. They may also indicate where and how psychometric tests could be helpful.
2. *Analyse the factors affecting decisions to join the organization.* These include:
   - the pay and total benefits package: this may have a considerable effect on decisions to join the organization but it is by no means the only factor; those set out below can be just as important, even more significant for some people:
   - career opportunities;
   - the opportunity to use existing skills or to acquire new skills;
   - the opportunity to use the latest technology and equipment, with which the organization is well supplied (of particular interest to research scientists and engineers);
   - access to high-level training;
   - a responsible and intrinsically rewarding job;
   - a belief that what the organization is doing is worthwhile;
   - the reputation of the organization as an employer;
   - the opportunity the job will provide to further the individual's career, for example the scope to achieve and have achievements recognized, increase in employability, or a respected company name to put on a CV.

3. *Competitive resourcing.* This will start from an analysis of the basis upon which the organization competes with other firms for employees. The factors mentioned above should be covered, and the aim is to seek competitive advantage by exploiting those that are superior to those of rivals. One of the factors will be pay. This may not be the only one but it can be important. It is necessary to track market rates and make a policy decision on where the organization wants to be in relation to the market.

4. *Alternative strategies for satisfying human resource requirements.* These consist of outsourcing, re-engineering, increasing flexibility skills training, multiskilling and downsizing.

5. *Recruitment and selection techniques.* The strategy should explore methods not only of recruiting the number of people required but also of finding staff who have the necessary skills and experience, who are likely to deliver the desired sort of behaviour and who will fit into the organization's culture readily. These processes and techniques will include the use of:
   - skills analysis;
   - competency mapping;
   - the internet for recruitment;
   - biodata;
   - structured interviews;
   - psychometric testing;
   - assessment centres.

The aim of the strategy is to develop the best mix of recruitment and selection tools. It has been demonstrated that a 'bundle' of selection techniques is likely to be more effective as a method of predicting the likely success of candidates than relying on a single method such as an interview.

RETENTION STRATEGY

Retention strategies aim to ensure that key people stay with the organization and that wasteful and expensive levels of employee turnover are reduced. They will be based on an analysis of why people stay and why they leave.

Analysis of reasons for staying or leaving

The reasons why people remain with the organization can be established through attitude surveys. These could segment respondents according to their length of service and analyse the answers of longer-serving employees to establish if there are any common patterns. The survey results could be supplemented by focus groups, which would discuss why people stay and identify any problems.

An analysis of why people leave through exit interviews may provide some information, but they are unreliable – people rarely give the full reasons why they are going. A better method is to conduct attitude surveys at regular intervals. The retention plan should address each of the areas in which lack of commitment and dissatisfaction can arise. The actions to be considered under each heading are listed below.

Pay

Problems arise because of uncompetitive, inequitable or unfair pay systems. Possible actions include:

∎ reviewing pay levels on the basis of market surveys;
∎ introducing job evaluation or improving an existing scheme to provide for equitable grading decisions;
∎ ensuring that employees understand the link between performance and reward;
∎ reviewing performance-related pay schemes to ensure that they operate fairly;
∎ adapting payment-by-results systems to ensure that employees are not penalized when they are engaged only on short runs;
∎ tailoring benefits to individual requirements and preference;
∎ involving employees in developing and operating job evaluation and contingent pay systems.

Job design

Dissatisfaction results if jobs are unrewarding in themselves. Jobs should be designed to maximize skill variety, task significance, autonomy and feedback, and they should provide opportunities for learning and growth.

Performance

Employees can be demotivated if they are unclear about their responsibilities or performance standards, are uninformed about how well they are doing, or feel that their performance assessments are unfair. The following actions can be taken:

∎ express performance requirements in terms of hard but attainable goals;
∎ get employees and managers to agree on those goals and the steps required to achieve them;

- encourage managers to praise employees for good performance but also get them to provide regular, informative and easily interpreted feedback – performance problems should be discussed as they happen in order that immediate corrective action can be taken;
- train managers in performance review techniques such as counselling;
- brief employees on how the performance management system works and obtain feedback from them on how it has been applied.

Learning and development

Resignations and turnover can increase if people are not given opportunities for learning and development, or feel that demands are being made upon them that they cannot reasonably be expected to fulfil without proper training. New employees can go through an 'induction crisis' if they are not given adequate training when they join the organization. Learning and development programmes should be developed and introduced that:

- give employees the competence and confidence to achieve expected performance standards;
- enhance existing skills and competencies;
- help people to acquire new skills and competencies so that they can make better use of their abilities, take on greater responsibilities, undertake a greater variety of tasks and earn more under skill- and competency-based pay schemes;
- ensure that new employees quickly acquire and learn the basic skills and knowledge needed to make a good start in their jobs;
- increase employability, inside and outside the organization.

Career development

Dissatisfaction with career prospects is a major cause of turnover. To a certain extent, this has to be accepted. More and more people recognize that to develop their careers they need to move on, and there is little their employers can do about it, especially in today's flatter organizations where promotion prospects are more limited. These are the individuals who acquire a 'portfolio' of skills and may consciously change direction several times during their careers. To a certain degree, employers should welcome this tendency. The idea of providing 'cradle to grave' careers is no longer as relevant in the more changeable job markets of today, and this self-planned, multiskilling process provides for the availability of a greater number of qualified people. But there is still everything to be said in most organizations for maintaining a stable core workforce, and in this situation employers should still plan to provide career opportunities by:

▌ providing employees with wider experience;
▌ introducing more systematic procedures for identifying potential, such as assessment or development centres;
▌ encouraging promotion from within;
▌ developing more equitable promotion procedures;
▌ providing advice and guidance on career paths.

Commitment

This can be increased by:

▌ explaining the organization's mission, values and strategies and encouraging employees to discuss and comment on them;
▌ communicating with employees in a timely and candid way, with the emphasis on face-to-face communications through such means as briefing groups;
▌ constantly seeking and taking into account the views of people at work;
▌ providing opportunities for employees to contribute their ideas on improving work systems;
▌ introducing organization and job changes only after consultation and discussion.

Lack of group cohesion

Employees can feel isolated and unhappy if they are not part of a cohesive team or if they are bedevilled by disruptive power politics. Steps can be taken to tackle this problem through teamwork (setting up self-managing or autonomous work groups or project teams) or team building (emphasizing the importance of teamwork as a key value and rewarding people for working effectively as members of teams and developing teamwork skills).

Dissatisfaction and conflict with managers and supervision

A common reason for resignations is the feeling that management in general, or individual managers and team leaders in particular, are not providing the leadership they should, are treating people unfairly or are bullying their staff (not an uncommon situation). As the saying goes, people tend to leave their managers, not the organization. This problem should be remedied by:

▌ selecting managers and team leaders with well-developed leadership qualities;
▌ training them in leadership skills and in methods of resolving conflict and dealing with grievances;

∎ introducing better procedures for handling grievances and disciplinary problems, and training everyone in how to use them.

Recruitment, selection and promotion

Rapid turnover can result simply from poor selection or promotion decisions. It is essential to ensure that selection and promotion procedures match the capacities of individuals to the demands of the work they have to do.

Over-marketing

Creating unrealistic expectations about career development opportunities, tailored training programmes, increasing employability and varied and interesting work can, if not matched with reality, lead directly to dissatisfaction and early resignation. Care should be taken not to oversell the firm's employee development policies. This can be achieved by using realistic previews as part of the selection process.

FLEXIBILITY STRATEGY

The aims of the flexibility strategy should be to develop a 'flexible firm' (Atkinson, 1984) by providing for greater operational and role flexibility.

The steps to be considered when formulating a flexibility strategy are as follows:

∎ Take a radical look at traditional employment patterns to find alternatives to full-time, permanent staff. This may take the form of segregating the workforce into a 'core group' and one or more peripheral groups.
∎ Think about outsourcing – getting work done by external firms or individuals.
∎ Encourage multiskilling to increase the ability of people to switch jobs or carry out any of the tasks that have to be undertaken by their team.

15

Talent management strategy

In this chapter 1) talent management and the concept of talent are defined, 2) the process of talent management is explained and 3) the approach to developing a talent management strategy is described.

TALENT MANAGEMENT DEFINED

Talent management is basically about the identification and development of potential. It can be defined more elaborately as the process of identifying, developing, recruiting, retaining and deploying talented people. The term talent management may refer simply to management succession planning and management development activities, although this notion does not really add anything to these familiar processes except a new, although admittedly quite evocative, name. It is better to regard talent management as a more comprehensive and integrated bundle of activities, the aim of which is to secure the flow of talent in an organization, bearing in mind that talent is a major corporate resource. But to understand the process of talent management it is necessary to be clear about what is meant by 'talent'.

What is talent?

As defined by the CIPD (2007b), 'Talent consists of those individuals who can make a difference to organizational performance, either through their immediate contribution or in the longer term by demonstrating the highest levels of potential.'

There are different views about what talent means. Some follow the lead given by McKinsey & Company, which coined the phrase 'the war for talent' in 1997. A book on this subject by Michaels *et al* (2001) identified five impera- tives that companies need to act on if they are going to win the war for mana- gerial talent. These are:

1. creating a winning employee value proposition that will make your company uniquely attractive to talent;
2. moving beyond recruiting hype to build a long-term recruiting strategy;
3. using job experience, coaching and mentoring to cultivate the potential in managers;
4. strengthening your talent pool by investing in A players, developing B players and acting decisively on C players;
5. having a pervasive mindset, which is central to this approach – a deep conviction shared by leaders throughout the company that competitive advantage comes from having better talent at all levels.

The McKinsey prescription has often been misinterpreted to mean that talent management is only about obtaining, identifying and nurturing high-flyers, ignoring the point they made that competitive advantage comes from having better talent at all levels.

Jeffrey Pfeffer (2001) has doubts about the war for talent concept, which he thinks is the wrong metaphor for organizational success. He believes that:

> Fighting the war for talent itself can cause problems. Companies that adopt a talent war mind-set often wind up venerating outsiders and downplaying the talent already in the company. They frequently set up competitive zero-sum dynamics that make internal learning and knowledge transfer difficult, activate the self-fulfilling prophecy in the wrong direction (those labelled as less able become less able), and create an attitude of arrogance instead of an attitude of wisdom. For all these reasons, fighting the war for talent may be hazardous to an organization's health and detrimental to doing the things that will make it successful.

HR people also have different views, which state on the one hand that everyone has talent and it not just about the favoured few, and on the other that you need to focus on the best. As reported by Warren (2006), Laura Ashley, director of talent at newspaper group Metro, believes you must maximize the performance of your workforce as a whole if you are going to maximize the performance of the organization. Alternatively, Wendy Hirsh, principal associate at the Institute for Employment Studies, says it is not helpful to confuse talent management with overall employee development.

Both are important, but talent management is best kept clear and focused. Another view was expressed by Thorne and Pellant (2007), who wrote: 'No organization should focus all its attention on development of only part of its human capital. What is important, however, is recognizing the needs of different individuals within its community.'

The general consensus seems to be that while talent management does focus on obtaining, identifying and developing people with high potential this should not be at the expense of the development needs of people generally.

THE PROCESS OF TALENT MANAGEMENT

Talent management takes the form of a 'bundle' of interrelated processes as shown in Figure 15.1.

Talent management starts with the business strategy and what it signifies in terms of the talented people required by the organization. Ultimately, its aim is to develop and maintain a pool of talented people. Its elements are described below.

The resourcing strategy

The business plan provides the basis for human resource planning, which defines human capital requirements and leads to attraction and retention policies and programmes for internal resourcing (identifying talented people within the organization and developing and promoting them).

Attraction and retention policies and programmes

These policies and programmes describe the approach to ensuring that the organization both gets and keeps the talent it needs. Attraction policies lead to programmes for external resourcing (recruitment and selection of people from outside the organization). Retention policies are designed to ensure that people remain as committed members of the organization. The outcome of these policies is a talent flow that creates and maintains the talent pool.

Talent audit

A talent audit identifies those with potential and provides the basis for career planning and development – ensuring that talented people have the sequence of experience supplemented by coaching and learning programmes that will fit them to carry out more demanding roles in the

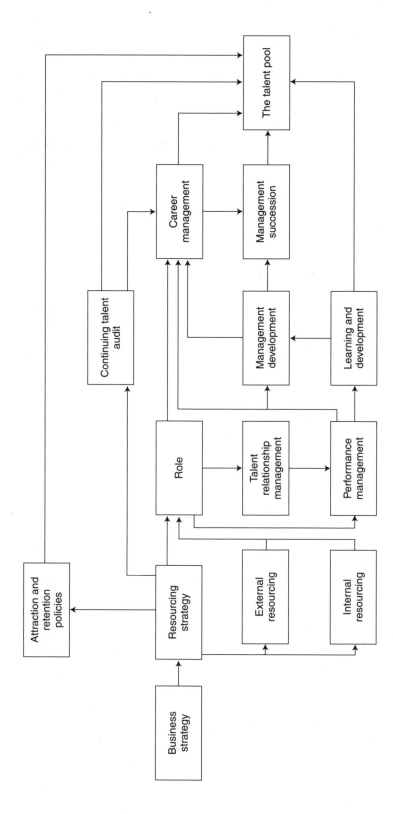

Figure 15.1 The elements of talent management

future. Talent audits can also be used to indicate the possible danger of talented people leaving (risk analysis) and what action may need to be taken to retain them.

Role

Talent management is concerned with the roles people carry out. This involves role design – ensuring that roles provide the responsibility, challenge and autonomy required to create role engagement and motivation. It also means taking steps to ensure that people have the opportunity and are given the encouragement to learn and develop in their roles. Talent management policies focus on role flexibility – giving people the chance to develop their roles by making better and extended use of their talents.

Talent relationship management

Talent relationship management is the process of building effective relationships with people in their roles. It is concerned generally with creating a great place to work, but in particular it is about treating individual employees fairly, recognizing their value, giving them a voice and providing opportunities for growth. The aim is to achieve 'talent engagement', ensuring that people are committed to their work and the organization. As Sears (2003) points out, it is 'better to build an existing relationship rather than try to create a new one when someone leaves'.

Performance management

Performance management processes provide a means of building relationships with people, identifying talent and potential, planning learning and development activities and making the most of the talent possessed by the organization. Line managers can be asked to carry out separate 'risk analyses' for any key staff to assess the likelihood of their leaving. Properly carried out, performance management is a means of increasing the engagement and motivation of people by providing positive feedback and recognition. This is part of a total reward system.

Learning and development

Learning and development policies and programmes are essential components in the process of talent management – ensuring that people acquire and enhance the skills and competencies they need. Policies should be formulated by reference to 'employee success profiles', which are described in terms of competencies and define the qualities that need to be developed.

Employee success profiles can be incorporated in role profiles.

Career management

Career management consists of the processes of career planning and management succession. Career planning shapes the progression of individuals within an organization in accordance with assessments of organizational needs, defined employee success profiles, and the performance, potential and preferences of individual members of the enterprise. As reported by Ready and Conger (2007), at Procter & Gamble 'destination jobs' are identified for high-potentials, which are attainable only if the employee continues to perform, impress and demonstrate growth potential.

Management succession planning takes place to ensure that, as far as possible, the organization has the managers it requires to meet future business needs.

DEVELOPING A TALENT MANAGEMENT STRATEGY

A talent management strategy consists of a view on how the processes described above should mesh together with an overall objective – to acquire and nurture talent wherever it is and wherever it is needed by using a number of interdependent policies and practices. Talent management is the notion of 'bundling' in action.

Components of a talent management strategy

A talent management strategy involves:

- defining who the talent management programme should cover;
- defining what is meant by talent in terms of competencies and potential;
- defining the future talent requirements of the organization;
- developing the organization as an 'employer of choice' – a 'great place to work';
- using selection and recruitment procedures that ensure that good-quality people are recruited who are likely to thrive in the organization and stay with it for a reasonable length of time (but not necessarily for life);
- designing jobs and developing roles that give people opportunities to apply and grow their skills and provide them with autonomy, interest and challenge;
- providing talented staff with opportunities for career development and growth;

▮ creating a working environment in which work processes and facilities enable rewarding (in the broadest sense) jobs and roles to be designed and developed;

▮ providing scope for achieving a reasonable balance between working in the organization and life outside work;

▮ developing a positive psychological contract;

▮ developing the leadership qualities of line managers;

▮ recognizing those with talent by rewarding excellence, enterprise and achievement;

▮ conducting talent audits that identify those with potential and those who might leave the organization;

▮ introducing management succession planning procedures that identify the talent available to meet future requirements and indicate what management development activities are required.

The qualities required

The development and implementation of a talent management strategy requires high-quality management and leadership from the top and from senior managers and the HR function. As suggested by Younger *et al* (2007), the approaches required involve emphasizing 'growth from within', regarding talent development as a key element of the business strategy, being clear about the competencies and qualities that matter, maintaining well-defined career paths, taking management development, coaching and mentoring very seriously, and demanding high performance.

16

Learning and development strategy

Learning and development strategies enable activities to be planned and implemented that ensure that the organization has the talented and skilled people it needs and that individuals are given the opportunity to enhance their knowledge and skills and levels of competency. They are the active components of an overall approach to strategic human resources development (strategic HRD) as described below. Learning and development strategies are concerned with developing a learning culture, promoting organizational learning, establishing a learning organization and providing for individual learning as also described in this chapter.

STRATEGIC HUMAN RESOURCE DEVELOPMENT (SHRD)

SHRD is defined by Walton (1999) as follows: 'Strategic human resource development involves introducing, eliminating, modifying, directing, and guiding processes in such a way that all individuals and teams are equipped with the skills, knowledge and competences they require to undertake current and future tasks required by the organization.'

As described by Harrison (2000), strategic HRD is 'development that arises from a clear vision about people's abilities and potential and operates within the overall strategic framework of the business'. Strategic HRD takes a broad and long-term view about how HRD policies and practices can support the achievement of business strategies. It is business-led, and the learning and development strategies that are established as part of the overall SHRD approach flow from business strategies, although they have a positive role in helping to ensure that the business attains its goals.

Strategic HRD aims

Strategic HRD aims to produce a coherent and comprehensive framework for developing people through the creation of a learning culture and the formulation of organizational and individual learning strategies. Its objective is to enhance resource capability in accordance with the belief that a firm's human resources are a major source of competitive advantage. It is therefore about developing the intellectual capital required by the organization as well as ensuring that the right quality of people is available to meet present and future needs. The main thrust of SHRD is to provide an environment in which people are encouraged to learn and develop. Although SHRD is business-led, its specific strategies have to take into account individual aspirations and needs. The importance of increasing employability outside as well as within the organization should be one of its concerns.

Strategic HRD policies are closely associated with that aspect of strategic HRM that is concerned with investing in people and developing the organization's human capital. As Keep (1989) says:

> One of the primary objectives of HRM is the creation of conditions whereby the latent potential of employees will be realized and their commitment to the causes of the organization secured. This latent potential is taken to include, not merely the capacity to acquire and utilize new skills and knowledge, but also a hitherto untapped wealth of ideas about how the organization's operations might be better ordered.

Human resource development philosophy

The philosophy underpinning strategic HRD is as follows:

▮ Human resource development makes a major contribution to the successful attainment of the organization's objectives, and investment in it benefits all the stakeholders of the organization.
▮ Human resource development plans and programmes should be integrated with and support the achievement of business and human resource strategies.

- Human resource development should always be performance-related – designed to achieve specified improvements in corporate, functional, team and individual performance and make a major contribution to bottom-line results.
- Everyone in the organization should be encouraged and given the opportunity to learn – to develop their skills and knowledge to the maximum of their capacity.
- The framework for individual learning is provided by personal development plans that focus on self-managed learning and are supported by coaching, mentoring and formal training.
- The organization needs to invest in learning and development by providing appropriate learning opportunities and facilities, but the prime responsibility for learning and development rests with individuals, who will be given the guidance and support of their managers and, as necessary, members of the HR department.

This involves creating a learning culture, the characteristics of which are self-managed learning not instruction, long-term capacity building not short-term fixes, and empowerment not supervision.

Elements of human resource development

The key elements of human resource development are:

- *Learning* – defined by Bass and Vaughan (1966) as 'a relatively permanent change in behaviour that occurs as a result of practice or experience'. As Kolb (1984) describes it, 'Learning is the major process of human adaptation.'
- *Training* – the planned and systematic modification of behaviour through learning events, programmes and instruction that enable individuals to achieve the levels of knowledge, skill and competence needed to carry out their work effectively.
- *Development* – the growth or realization of a person's ability and potential through the provision of learning and educational experiences.
- *Education* – the development of the knowledge, values and understanding required in all aspects of life rather than the knowledge and skills relating to particular areas of activity.

Learning should be distinguished from training. 'Learning is the process by which a person constructs new knowledge, skills and capabilities, whereas training is one of several responses an organization can undertake to promote learning' (Reynolds *et al*, 2002).

STRATEGIES FOR CREATING A LEARNING CULTURE

A learning culture is one in which learning is recognized by top management, line managers and employees generally as an essential organizational process to which they are committed and in which they engage continuously. It is described by Reynolds (2004) as a 'growth medium' that will 'encourage employees to commit to a range of positive discretionary behaviours, including learning' and that has the following characteristics: empowerment not supervision, self-managed learning not instruction, long-term capacity building not short-term fixes. Discretionary learning according to Sloman (2003) happens when individuals actively seek to acquire the knowledge and skills that promote the organization's objectives.

The steps required to create a learning culture as proposed by Reynolds (2004) are:

1. Develop and share the vision – belief in a desired and emerging future.
2. Empower employees – provide 'supported autonomy': freedom for employees to manage their work within certain boundaries (policies and expected behaviours) but with support available as required. Adopt a facilitative style of management in which responsibility for decision making is ceded as far as possible to employees.
3. Provide employees with a supportive learning environment where learning capabilities can be discovered and applied, eg peer networks, supportive policies and systems, and protected time for learning.
4. Use coaching techniques to draw out the talents of others by encouraging employees to identify options and seek their own solutions to problems.
5. Guide employees through their work challenges and provide them with time, resources and, crucially, feedback.
6. Recognize the importance of managers acting as role models: 'The new way of thinking and behaving may be so different that you must see what it looks like before you can imagine yourself doing it. You must see the new behaviour and attitudes in others with whom you can identify' (Schein, 1990).
7. Encourage networks – communities of practice.
8. Align systems to vision – get rid of bureaucratic systems that produce problems rather than facilitate work.

ORGANIZATIONAL LEARNING STRATEGIES

Organizations can be described as continuous learning systems, and organizational learning has been defined by Marsick (1994) as a process of 'Co-ordinated systems change, with mechanisms built in for individuals and groups to access, build and use organizational memory, structure and culture to develop long-term organizational capacity'.

Organizational learning strategy aims to develop a firm's resource-based capability. This is in accordance with one of the basic principles of human resource management, namely that it is necessary to invest in people in order to develop the human capital required by the organization and to increase its stock of knowledge and skills. As stated by Ehrenberg and Smith (1994), human capital theory indicates that 'The knowledge and skills a worker has – which comes from education and training, including the training that experience brings – generate a certain stock of productive capital.'

Five principles of organizational learning have been defined by Harrison (1997):

1. The need for a powerful and cohering vision of the organization to be communicated and maintained across the workforce in order to promote awareness of the need for strategic thinking at all levels.
2. The need to develop strategy in the context of a vision that is not only powerful but also open-ended and unambiguous. This will encourage a search for a wide rather than a narrow range of strategic options, will promote lateral thinking and will orient the knowledge-creating activities of employees.
3. Within the framework of vision and goals, frequent dialogue, communication and conversations are major facilitators of organizational learning.
4. It is essential continuously to challenge people to re-examine what they take for granted.
5. It is essential to develop a conducive learning and innovation climate.

Single- and double-loop learning

Argyris (1992) suggests that organizational learning occurs under two conditions: first, when an organization achieves what is intended and, second, when a mismatch between intentions and outcomes is identified and corrected. But organizations do not perform the actions that produce the learning; it is individual members of the organization who behave in ways that lead to it, although organizations can create conditions that facilitate such learning.

Argyris distinguishes between single-loop and double-loop learning. Single-loop learning organizations define the 'governing variables', ie what they expect to achieve in terms of targets and standards. They then monitor and review achievements, and take corrective action as necessary, thus completing the loop. Double-loop learning occurs when the monitoring process initiates action to redefine the 'governing variables' to meet the new situation, which may be imposed by the external environment. The organization has learnt something new about what has to be achieved in the light of changed circumstances and can then decide how this should be achieved.

LEARNING ORGANIZATION STRATEGY

The process of organizational learning is related to the concept of a learning organization, which Senge (1990) describes as an 'organization that is continually expanding to create its future'. It has been defined by Wick and Leon (1995) as an organization that 'continually improves by rapidly creating and refining the capabilities required for future success', and by Pedler *et al* (1989) as an organization that 'facilitates the learning of all its members and continually transforms itself'. As Burgoyne (1994) has pointed out, learning organizations have to be able to adapt to their context and develop their people to match the context.

Garvin (1993) suggests that learning organizations are good at doing five things:

1. *Systematic problem solving*, which rests heavily on the philosophy and methods of the quality movement. Its underlying ideas include relying on scientific method, rather than guesswork, for diagnosing problems – what Deming (1986) calls the 'plan–do–check–act' cycle and others refer to as 'hypothesis-generating, hypothesis-testing' techniques. Data rather than assumptions are required as the background to decision making – what quality practitioners call 'fact-based management', and simple statistical tools such as histograms, Pareto charts and cause-and-effect diagrams are used to organize data and draw inferences.
2. *Experimentation* – this activity involves the systematic search for and testing of new knowledge. Continuous improvement programmes – 'kaizen' – are an important feature in a learning organization.
3. *Learning from past experience* – learning organizations review their successes and failures, assess them systematically and record the lessons learnt in a way that employees find open and accessible. This process has been called the 'Santayana principle', quoting the philosopher George Santayana, who coined the phrase 'Those who cannot remember the past are condemned to repeat it.'
4. *Learning from others* – sometimes the most powerful insights come from looking outside one's immediate environment to gain a new perspective. This process has been called SIS for 'steal ideas shamelessly'. Another

more acceptable word for it is benchmarking – a disciplined process of identifying best-practice organizations and analysing the extent to which what they are doing can be transferred, with suitable modifications, to one's own environment.

5. *Transferring knowledge quickly and efficiently throughout the organization* by seconding people with new expertise, or by education and training programmes, as long as the latter are linked explicitly with implementation.

One approach, as advocated by Senge (1990), is to focus on collective problem solving within an organization. This is achieved using team learning and a 'soft systems' methodology whereby all the possible causes of a problem are considered in order to define more clearly those that can be dealt with and those that are insoluble.

A learning organization strategy will be based on the belief that learning is a continuous process rather than a set of discrete training activities (Sloman, 1999). It will incorporate strategies for organizational learning as described above and individual learning as discussed below.

INDIVIDUAL LEARNING STRATEGIES

The individual learning strategies of an organization are driven by its human resource requirements, the latter being expressed in terms of the sort of skills and behaviours that will be required to achieve business goals. The starting point should be the approaches adopted to the provision of learning and development opportunities, bearing in mind the distinction between learning and development made by Pedler, Boydell and Burgoyne (1989), who see learning as being concerned with an increase in knowledge or a higher degree of an existing skill, whereas development is more towards a different state of being or functioning. Sloman (2003) points out that:

Interventions and activities which are intended to improve knowledge and skills will increasingly focus on the learner. Emphasis will shift to the individual learner (or team). And he or she will be encouraged to take more responsibility for his or her learning. Efforts will be made to develop a climate which supports effective and appropriate learning. Such interventions and activities will form part of an integrated approach to creating competitive advantage through people in the organization.

The learning strategy should cover:

▮ how learning needs will be identified;
▮ the role of personal development planning and self-managed learning;
▮ the support that should be provided for individual learning in the form of guidance, coaching, learning resource centres, mentoring, external courses designed to meet the particular needs of individuals, internal or external training programmes and courses designed to meet the needs of groups of employees.

17

Reward strategy

REWARD STRATEGY DEFINED

Reward strategy is a declaration of intent that defines what the organization wants to do in the longer term to develop and implement reward policies, practices and processes that will further the achievement of its business goals and meet the needs of its stakeholders.

Reward strategy provides a sense of purpose and direction and a framework for developing reward policies, practices and processes. It is based on an understanding of the needs of the organization *and* its employees and how they can best be satisfied. It is also concerned with developing the values of the organization on how people should be rewarded and formulating guiding principles that will ensure that these values are enacted.

Reward strategy is underpinned by a reward philosophy, which expresses what the organization believes should be the basis upon which people are valued and rewarded. Reward philosophies are often articulated as guiding principles.

WHY HAVE A REWARD STRATEGY?

Overall, in the words of Duncan Brown (2001), 'Reward strategy is ultimately a way of thinking that you can apply to any reward issue arising in your organization, to see how you can create value from it.' More specifically, there are four arguments for developing reward strategies:

1. You must have some idea where you are going, or how do you know how to get there, and how do you know that you have arrived (if you ever do)?
2. Pay costs in most organizations are by far the largest item of expense – they can be 60 per cent and often much more in labour-intensive organizations – so doesn't it make sense to think about how they should be managed and invested in the longer term?
3. There can be a positive relationship between rewards, in the broadest sense, and performance, so shouldn't we think about how we can strengthen that link?
4. As Cox and Purcell (1998) write, 'the real benefit in reward strategies lies in complex linkages with other human resource management policies and practices'. Isn't this a good reason for developing a reward strategic framework that indicates how reward processes will be linked to HR processes so that they are coherent and mutually supportive?

CHARACTERISTICS OF REWARD STRATEGIES

As Murlis (1996) points out, 'Reward strategy will be characterised by diversity and conditioned both by the legacy of the past and the realities of the future.' All reward strategies are different, just as all organizations are different. Of course, similar aspects of reward will be covered in the strategies of different organizations but they will be treated differently in accordance with variations between organizations in their contexts, strategies and cultures.

Reward strategists may have a clear idea of what needs to be done but they have to take account of the views of top management and be prepared to persuade them with convincing arguments that action needs to be taken. They have to take particular account of financial considerations – the concept of 'affordability' looms large in the minds of chief executives and financial directors, who will need to be convinced that an investment in rewards will pay off. They also have to convince employees and their representatives that the reward strategy will meet their needs as well as business needs.

THE STRUCTURE OF REWARD STRATEGY

Reward strategy should be based on a detailed analysis of the present arrangements for reward, which includes a statement of their strengths and weaknesses. This could take the form of a 'gap analysis', which compares what it is believed should be happening with what *is* happening and indicates which 'gaps' need to be filled. A format for the analysis is shown in Table 17.1.

A diagnosis should be made of the reasons for any gaps or problems so that decisions can be made on what needs to be done to overcome them. It can then be structured under the headings set out below:

1. *A statement of intentions* – the reward initiatives that it is proposed should be taken.
2. *A rationale* – the reasons why the proposals are being made. The rationale should make out the business case for the proposals, indicating how they will meet business needs and setting out the costs and the benefits. It should also refer to any people issues that need to be addressed and how the strategy will deal with them.
3. *A plan* – how, when and by whom the reward initiatives will be implemented. The plan should indicate what steps will need to be taken and should take account of resource constraints and the need for communications, involvement and training. The priorities attached to each element of the strategy should be indicated and a timetable for implementation should be drawn up. The plan should state who will be responsible for the development and implementation of the strategy.
4. *A definition of guiding principles* – the values that it is believed should be adopted in formulating and implementing the strategy.

THE CONTENT OF REWARD STRATEGY

Reward strategy may be a broad-brush affair simply indicating the general direction in which it is thought reward management should go. Additionally or alternatively, reward strategy may set out a list of specific intentions dealing with particular aspects of reward management.

Broad-brush reward strategy

A broad-brush reward strategy may commit the organization to the pursuit of a total rewards policy. The basic aim might be to achieve an appropriate balance between financial and non-financial rewards. A further aim could be to use other approaches to the development of the employment relationship and the work environment that will enhance commitment and engagement and provide more opportunities for the contribution of people to be valued and recognized.

Table 17.1 A reward gap analysis

What Should Be Happening	What Is Happening	What Needs To Be Done
1. A total reward approach is adopted that emphasizes the significance of both financial and non-financial rewards.		
2. Reward policies and practices are developed within the framework of a well-articulated strategy that is designed to support the achievement of business objectives and meet the needs of stakeholders.		
3. A job evaluation scheme is used that properly reflects the values of the organization, is up to date with regard to the jobs it covers and is non-discriminatory.		
4. Equal pay issues are given serious attention. This includes the conduct of equal pay reviews that lead to action.		
5. Market rates are tracked carefully so that a competitive pay structure exists that contributes to the attraction and retention of high-quality people.		
6. Grade and pay structures are based on job evaluation and market rate analysis, appropriate to the characteristics and needs of the organization and its employees, facilitate the management of relativities, provide scope for rewarding contribution, clarify reward and career opportunities, are constructed logically, operate transparently and are easy to manage and maintain.		
7. Contingent pay schemes reward contribution fairly and consistently, support the motivation of staff and the development of a performance culture, deliver the right messages about the values of the organization, contain a clear 'line of sight' between contribution and reward and are cost-effective.		

8. Performance management processes contribute to performance improvement, people development and the management of expectations, operate effectively throughout the organization and are supported by line managers and staff.		
9. Employee benefits and pension schemes meet the needs of stakeholders and are cost-effective.		
10. A flexible benefits approach is adopted.		
11. Reward management procedures exist that ensure that reward processes are managed effectively and that costs are controlled.		
12. Appropriate use is made of computers (software and spreadsheets) to assist in the process of reward management.		
13. Reward management aims and arrangements are transparent and communicated well to staff.		
14. Surveys are used to assess the opinions of staff about reward, and action is taken on the outcomes.		
15. An appropriate amount of responsibility for reward is devolved to line managers.		
16. Line managers are capable of carrying out their devolved responsibilities well.		
17. Steps are taken to train line managers and provide them with support and guidance as required.		
18. HR has the knowledge and skills to provide the required reward management advice and services and to guide and support line managers.		
19. Overall, reward management developments are conscious of the need to achieve affordability and to demonstrate that they are cost-effective.		
20. Steps are taken to evaluate the effectiveness of reward management processes and to ensure that they reflect changing needs.		

Examples of other broad strategic aims include 1) introducing a more integrated approach to reward management – encouraging continuous personal development and spelling out career opportunities, 2) developing a more flexible approach to reward, which includes the reduction of artificial barriers as a result of overemphasis on grading and promotion, 3) generally rewarding people according to their contribution, 4) supporting the development of a performance culture and building levels of competence, and 5) clarifying what behaviours will be rewarded and why.

Specific reward initiatives

The selection of reward initiatives and the priorities attached to them will be based on an analysis of the present circumstances of the organization and an assessment of the needs of the business and its employees. The following are examples of possible specific reward initiatives, one or more of which might feature in a reward strategy:

- the replacement of present methods of contingent pay with a pay-for-contribution scheme;
- the introduction of a new grade and pay structure, eg a broad-graded or career family structure;
- the replacement of an existing decayed job evaluation scheme with a computerized scheme that more clearly reflects organizational values;
- the improvement of performance management processes so that they provide better support for the development of a performance culture and more clearly identify development needs;
- the introduction of a formal recognition scheme;
- the development of a flexible benefits system;
- the conduct of equal pay reviews with the objective of ensuring that work of equal value is paid equally;
- communication programmes designed to inform everyone of the reward policies and practices of the organization;
- training, coaching and guidance programmes designed to increase line management capability (see also 'Reward strategy and line management capability', page 192).

GUIDING PRINCIPLES

Guiding principles define the approach an organization takes to dealing with reward. They are the basis for reward policies and provide guidelines for the actions contained in the reward strategy. They express the reward philosophy of the organization – its values and beliefs about how people should be rewarded.

Members of the organization should be involved in the definition of guiding principles, which can then be communicated to everyone to increase understanding of what underpins reward policies and practices. However, employees will suspend their judgement of the principles until they experience how they are applied. What matters to them is not the philosophies themselves but the pay practices emanating from them and the messages about the employment 'deal' that they get as a consequence. It is the reality that is important, not the rhetoric.

Guiding principles should incorporate or be influenced by general beliefs about fairness, equity, consistency and transparency. They may be concerned with such specific matters as:

▌ developing reward policies and practices that support the achievement of business goals;
▌ providing rewards that attract, retain and motivate staff and help to develop a high-performance culture;
▌ maintaining competitive rates of pay;
▌ rewarding people according to their contribution;
▌ recognizing the value of all staff who are making an effective contribution, not just the exceptional performers;
▌ allowing a reasonable degree of flexibility in the operation of reward processes and in the choice of benefits by employees;
▌ devolving more responsibility for reward decisions to line managers.

DEVELOPING REWARD STRATEGY

The formulation of corporate strategy can be described as a process for developing and defining a sense of direction. There are four key development phases:

1. the *diagnosis* phase, when reward goals are agreed, current policies and practices assessed against them, options for improvement considered and any changes agreed;
2. the *detailed design* phase, when improvements and changes are detailed and any changes tested (pilot testing is important);
3. the final *testing and preparation* phase;
4. the *implementation* phase, followed by ongoing review and modification.

A logical step-by-step model for doing this is illustrated in Figure 17.1. This incorporates ample provision for consultation, involvement and

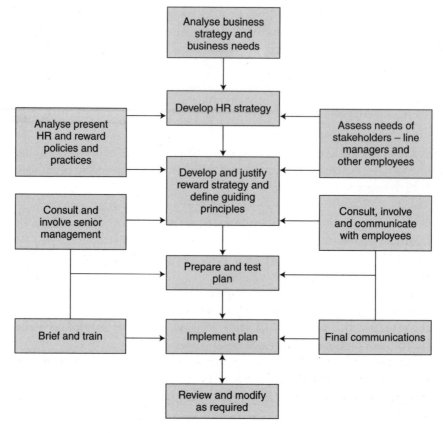

Figure 17.1 A model of the reward strategy development process

communication with stakeholders, who include senior managers as the ultimate decision makers as well as employees and line managers.

In practice, however, the formulation of reward strategy is seldom as logical and linear a process as this. Reward strategies evolve; they have to respond to changes in organizational requirements, which are happening all the time. They need to track emerging trends in reward management and may modify their views accordingly, as long as they do not leap too hastily on the latest bandwagon.

It may be helpful to set out reward strategies on paper for the record and as a basis for planning and communication. But this should be regarded as no more than a piece of paper that can be torn up when needs change – as they will – not a tablet of stone.

EFFECTIVE REWARD STRATEGIES

Components of an effective reward strategy

Duncan Brown (2001) has suggested that effective reward strategies have three components:

1. They have to have clearly defined goals and a well-defined link to business objectives.
2. There have to be well-designed pay and reward programmes, tailored to the needs of the organization and its people, and consistent and integrated with one another.
3. Perhaps most important and most neglected, there need to be effective and supportive HR and reward processes in place.

Criteria for effectiveness

The questions to be answered when assessing the effectiveness of a reward strategy as posed by Armstrong and Brown (2007) are:

1. Is it aligned with the organization's business strategy (vertical alignment or integration) and its HR strategies (horizontal alignment or integration)?
2. Will it support the achievement of business goals and reinforce organizational values and, if so, how?
3. Are the objectives of the reward strategy clearly defined, including a convincing statement of how the business needs of the organization will be met and how the needs of employees and other stakeholders will be catered for?
4. Is it based on a thorough analysis and diagnosis of the internal and external environment of the organization and the reward issues that need to be addressed?
5. Has a realistic assessment been made of the resources required to implement the strategy and the costs involved?
6. Is it affordable in the sense that the benefits will exceed any costs?
7. Have steps been taken to ensure that supporting processes such as performance management, communication and training are in place?
8. Is the programme for implementation realistic?
9. Have steps been taken to ensure that it is supported and understood by line managers and staff?
10. Will HR and line managers be capable of implementing and managing the strategy in practice?

11. Have accountability and ownership for the various reward policies and practices been clarified, defining what success looks like and how it will be measured? Are effective review mechanisms in place?
12. Is the reward strategy flexible in adjusting to take account of changes in the business and in the environment?

REWARD STRATEGY AND LINE MANAGEMENT CAPABILITY

HR can initiate new reward policies and practices, but it is the line that has the main responsibility for implementing them. The trend is, rightly, to devolve more responsibility for managing reward to line managers. Some will have the ability to respond to the challenge and opportunity; others will be incapable of carrying out this responsibility without close guidance from HR; some may never be able to cope. Managers may not always do what HR expects them to do and, if compelled to, they may be half-hearted about it. This puts a tremendous onus on HR and reward specialists to develop line management capability, to initiate processes that can readily be implemented by line managers, to promote understanding by communicating what is happening, why it is happening and how it will affect everyone, to provide guidance and help where required and to provide formal training as necessary.

18

Employee relations strategy

EMPLOYEE RELATIONS STRATEGY DEFINED

Employee relations strategies define the intentions of the organization about what needs to be done and what needs to be changed in the ways in which the organization manages its relationships with employees and their trade unions. Like all other aspects of HR strategy, employee relations strategies will flow from the business strategy but will also aim to support it. For example, if the business strategy is to concentrate on achieving competitive edge through innovation and the delivery of quality to its customers, the employee relations strategy may emphasize processes of involvement and participation, including the implementation of programmes for continuous improvement and total quality management. If, however, the strategy for competitive advantage, or even survival, is cost reduction, the employee relations strategy may concentrate on how this can be achieved by maximizing cooperation with the unions and employees and by minimizing detrimental effects on those employees and disruption to the organization.

Employee relations strategies should be distinguished from employee relations policies. Strategies are dynamic. They provide a sense of direction and give an answer to the question 'How are we going to get from here to there?' Employee relations policies are more about the here and now. They express 'the way things are done around here' as far as dealing with unions and employees is concerned. Of course, they will evolve, but this may not be a result of a strategic choice. It is when a deliberate decision is made to change policies that a strategy for achieving this change has to be formulated. Thus if the policy is to increase commitment the strategy could consider how this might be achieved by involvement and participation processes.

CONCERNS OF EMPLOYEE RELATIONS STRATEGY

Employee relations strategy will be concerned with how to:

▌ build stable and cooperative relationships with employees that minimize conflict;
▌ achieve commitment through employee involvement and communications processes;
▌ develop mutuality – a common interest in achieving the organization's goals through the development of organizational cultures based on shared values between management and employees.

STRATEGIC DIRECTIONS

The intentions expressed by employee relations strategies may direct the organization towards any of the following:

▌ changing forms of recognition, including single-union recognition, or de-recognition;
▌ changes in the form and content of procedural agreements;
▌ new bargaining structures, including decentralization or single-table bargaining;
▌ the achievement of increased levels of commitment through involvement or participation – giving employees a voice;
▌ deliberately bypassing trade union representatives to communicate directly with employees;
▌ increasing the extent to which management controls operations in such areas as flexibility;
▌ generally improving the employee relations climate in order to produce more harmonious and cooperative relationships;
▌ developing a 'partnership' with trade unions as described later in this chapter, recognizing that employees are stakeholders and that it is to the advantage of both parties to work together (this could be described as a unitarist strategy aiming at increasing mutual commitment).

THE BACKGROUND TO EMPLOYEE RELATIONS STRATEGIES

Four approaches to employee relations have been identified by Industrial Relations Services (1993):

1. *Adversarial* – the organization decides what it wants to do, and employees are expected to fit in. Employees only exercise power by refusing to cooperate.
2. *Traditional* – a good day-to-day working relationship but management proposes and the workforce reacts through its elected representatives.
3. *Partnership* – the organization involves employees in the drawing up and execution of organization policies, but retains the right to manage.
4. *Power sharing* – employees are involved in both day-to-day and strategic decision making.

Adversarial approaches are much less common than in the 1960s and 1970s. The traditional approach is still the most typical, but more interest is being expressed in partnership as discussed later in this chapter. Power sharing is rare.

Against the background of a preference for one of the four approaches listed above, employee relations strategy will be based on the philosophy of the organization on what sort of relationships between management and employees and their unions are wanted and how they should be handled. A partnership strategy will aim to develop and maintain a positive, productive, cooperative and trusting climate of employee relations.

THE HRM APPROACH TO EMPLOYEE RELATIONS

The philosophy of HRM has been translated into the following prescriptions, which constitute the HRM model for employee relations:

▌ a drive for commitment – winning the 'hearts and minds' of employees to get them to identify with the organization, to exert themselves more on its behalf and to remain with the organization, thus ensuring a return on their training and development;
▌ an emphasis on mutuality – getting the message across that 'we are all in this together' and that the interests of management and employees coincide (ie a unitarist approach);

▮ the organization of complementary forms of communication, such as team briefing, alongside traditional collective bargaining, ie approaching employees directly as individuals or in groups rather than through their representatives;

▮ a shift from collective bargaining to individual contracts;

▮ the use of employee involvement techniques such as quality circles or improvement groups;

▮ continuous pressure on quality – total quality management;

▮ increased flexibility in working arrangements, including multiskilling, to provide for the more effective use of human resources, sometimes accompanied by an agreement to provide secure employment for the 'core' workers;

▮ emphasis on teamwork;

▮ harmonization of terms and conditions for all employees.

The key contrasting dimensions of traditional industrial relations and HRM have been presented by Guest (1995) as shown in Table 18.1.

Guest notes that this model aims to support the achievement of the three main sources of competitive advantage identified by Porter (1985), namely innovation, quality and cost leadership. Innovation and quality strategies require employee commitment, while cost leadership strategies are believed by many managements to be only achievable without a union. Guest comments that 'The logic of a market-driven HRM strategy is that where high organizational commitment is sought, unions are irrelevant. Where cost advantage is the goal, unions and industrial relations systems appear to carry higher costs.'

An HRM approach is still possible if trade unions are recognized by the organization. In this case, the strategy might be to marginalize or at least sidestep them by dealing direct with employees through involvement and communications processes.

Table 18.1 Key dimensions of traditional industrial relations and HRM

Dimension	Industrial Relations	HRM
Psychological contract	Compliance	Commitment
Behaviour references	Norms, custom, practice	Values, mission
Relations	Low trust, pluralist, collective	High trust, unitarist, individual
Organization design	Formal roles, hierarchy, division of labour, managerial control	Flexible roles, flat structure, teamwork and autonomy, self-control

Source: Guest (1995)

POLICY OPTIONS

There are a number of policy options that need to be considered when developing employee relations strategy. The following four options have been described by Guest (1995):

1. *The new realism – a high emphasis on HRM and industrial relations.* The aim is to integrate HRM and industrial relations. This is the policy of such organizations as Rover, Nissan and Toshiba. A review of new collaborative arrangements in the shape of single-table bargaining (IRS, 1993) found that they were almost always the result of employer initiatives, but that both employers and unions seem satisfied with them. They have facilitated greater flexibility, more multiskilling, the removal of demarcations and improvements in quality. They can also extend consultation processes and accelerate moves towards single status.
2. *Traditional collectivism – priority to industrial relations without HRM.* This involves retaining the traditional pluralist industrial relations arrangements within an eventually unchanged industrial relations system. Management may take the view in these circumstances that it is easier to continue to operate with a union, since it provides a useful, well-established channel for communication and for the handling of grievance, discipline and safety issues.
3. *Individualized HRM – high priority to HRM with no industrial relations.* According to Guest, this approach is not very common, except in North American-owned firms. It is, he believes, 'essentially piecemeal and opportunistic'.
4. *The black hole – no industrial relations.* This option is becoming more prevalent in organizations in which HRM is not a policy priority for managements but where they do not see that there is a compelling reason to operate within a traditional industrial relations system. When such organizations are facing a decision on whether or not to recognize a union, they are increasingly deciding not to do so.

FORMULATING EMPLOYEE RELATIONS STRATEGIES

Like other business and HR strategies, those concerned with employee relations can, in Mintzberg's (1987) words, 'emerge in response to an evolving situation'. But it is still useful to spend time deliberately formulating strategies, and the aim should be to create a shared agenda that will communicate a common perspective on what needs to be done. This can be expressed in writing, but it can also be clarified through involvement and communication processes. A partnership agreement may well be the best way of getting employee relations strategies into action.

PARTNERSHIP AGREEMENTS

Defined

In industrial relations a partnership arrangement can be described as one in which both parties (management and the trade union) agree to work together to their mutual advantage and to achieve a climate of more cooperative and therefore less adversarial industrial relations. A partnership agreement may include undertakings from both sides; for example management may offer job security linked to productivity and the union may agree to new forms of work organization that might require more flexibility on the part of employees.

Key values

Five key values for partnership have been set down by Roscow and Casner-Lotto (1998):

1. mutual trust and respect;
2. a joint vision for the future and the means to achieve it;
3. continuous exchange of information;
4. recognition of the central role of collective bargaining;
5. devolved decision making.

Their research in the United States indicated that, if these matters were addressed successfully by management and unions, then companies could expect productivity gains, quality improvements, a better-motivated and committed workforce and lower absenteeism and turnover rates.

The impact of partnership

The Department of Trade and Industry and Department for Education and Employment report on partnerships at work (1997) concludes that partnership is central to the strategy of successful organizations. A growing understanding that organizations must focus on customer needs has brought with it the desire to engage the attitudes and commitment of all employees in order to meet those needs effectively, says the report.

The report was based on interviews with managers and employees in 67 private and public sector organizations identified as 'innovative and successful'. It reveals how such organizations achieve significantly enhanced business performance through developing a partnership with their employees.

There are five main themes or 'paths' that the organizations identified as producing a balanced environment in which employees thrived and sought success for themselves and their organizations:

1. *Shared goals – 'understanding the business we are in'*. All employees should be involved in developing the organization's vision, resulting in a shared direction and enabling people to see how they fit into the organization and the contribution they are making. Senior managers in turn receive ideas from those who really understand the problems – and the opportunities.

2. *Shared culture – 'agreed values binding us together'*. In the research, 'organization after organization acknowledged that a culture has to build up over time… it cannot be imposed by senior executives but must rather be developed in an atmosphere of fairness, trust and respect until it permeates every activity of the organization'. Once achieved, a shared culture means that employees feel respected and so give of their best.

3. *Shared learning – 'continuously improving ourselves'*. Key business benefits of shared learning include an increasing receptiveness to change, and the benefits of increased organization loyalty brought by career and personal development plans.

4. *Shared effort – 'one business driven by flexible teams'*. Change has become such an important part of our daily lives that organizations have learnt that they cannot deal with it in an unstructured way, says the report. The response to change cannot be purely reactive, as business opportunities may be missed. While teamworking 'leads to essential co-operation across the whole organization', care must be taken to ensure that teams do not compete with each other in a counterproductive way. It is essential that the organization develops an effective communication system to ensure that the flow of information from and to teams enhances their effectiveness.

5. *Shared information – 'effective communication throughout the enterprise'*. While most organizations work hard at downward communication, the most effective communication of all 'runs up, down and across the business in a mixture of formal systems and informal processes'. Many organizations with unions have built successful relationships with them, developing key partnership roles in the effective dissemination of information, communication and facilitation of change, while others have found representative works councils useful in consulting employees and providing information.

Moving on

An important point that emerged from the research is that there are three levels, or stages, within each of these five paths. These are the levels 'at which certain elements of good practice must be established before the organization moves forward to break new ground'.

EMPLOYEE VOICE STRATEGIES

As defined by Boxall and Purcell (2003), 'Employee voice is the term increasingly used to cover a whole variety of processes and structures which enable, and sometimes empower employees, directly and indirectly, to contribute to decision-making in the firm.' Employee voice can be seen as 'the ability of employees to influence the actions of the employer' (Millward *et al*, 2000). The concept covers the provision of opportunities for employees to register discontent and modify the power of management. It embraces involvement and, more significantly, participation.

The framework for employee voice

The framework for employee voice strategies has been modelled by Marchington *et al* (2001) as shown in Figure 18.1.

This framework identifies two dimensions of voice: 1) individual employees; and 2) collective – union and other representation. The shared

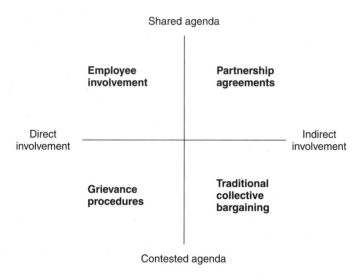

Figure 18.1 A framework for employee voice

agenda of involvement and partnership is a form of upward problem solving. This is on the same axis as the contested agenda of grievances and collective bargaining. But these are not absolutes. Organizations will have tendencies towards shared or contested agendas, just as there will be varying degrees of direct and indirect involvement, although they are unlikely to have partnership and traditional collective bargaining at the same time. As Kochan, Katz and McKersie (1986) point out, among the strongest factors affecting the choice of employee voice strategy are the values of management towards unions.

Planning for voice

The employee voice strategy appropriate for an organization depends upon the values and attitudes of management and, if they exist, trade unions, and the current climate of employee relations. Strategic planning should be based on a review of the existing forms of voice, which would include discussions with stakeholders (line managers, employees and trade union representatives) on the effectiveness of existing arrangements and any improvements required. In the light of these discussions, new or revised approaches can be developed, but it is necessary to brief and train those involved in the part they should play.

Part 4

The strategic HR toolkit

19

Strategic human resource management toolkit

The purpose of the toolkit is to provide the basis for conducting a strategic review of human resource management practices in order to develop and implement strategic human resource management. The individual tools can serve as checklists to analyse different aspects of HR strategy. They can also be used to involve people in the formulation of strategy by prompting discussions in workshops and focus groups. The kit consists of the following tools:

- *Tool 1:* Overall business analysis and HR implications;
- *Tool 2:* Analysis of competitive strategy and its implications;
- *Tool 3:* Analysis of business strategies and their implications;
- *Tool 4:* Analysis of fit between type of organization and HR strategy;
- *Tool 5:* 'Best-practice' analysis;
- *Tool 6:* Overall analysis of HR strategic goals;
- *Tool 7:* Overall strategic HRM gap analysis;
- *Tool 8:* Integration of business and HR strategies;
- *Tool 9:* Bundling of HR activities;
- *Tool 10:* Analysis of high-performance goals;
- *Tool 11:* High-performance work system gap analysis;
- *Tool 12:* Analysis of engagement and commitment levels – survey;
- *Tool 13:* Analysis of employee engagement goals;

▮ *Tool 14:* Employee engagement gap analysis;
▮ *Tool 15:* Analysis of resourcing goals;
▮ *Tool 16:* Resourcing gap analysis;
▮ *Tool 17:* Analysis of talent management goals;
▮ *Tool 18:* Talent management gap analysis;
▮ *Tool 19:* Analysis of learning and development goals;
▮ *Tool 20:* Gap analysis of learning and development activities;
▮ *Tool 21:* Analysis of reward management goals;
▮ *Tool 22:* Gap analysis of reward management activities;
▮ *Tool 23:* Analysis of employee relations goals;
▮ *Tool 24:* Gap analysis of employee relations activities.

Tool 1 Overall business analysis and HR implications

Business Matters		Human Resource Implications	
What business are we in?		What sort of people do we need in the business?	
Where are we going?		What sort of organization do we need to get there?	
What are our strengths, weaknesses, opportunities and threats?		To what extent are these strengths and weaknesses related to our HR capability?	
		What opportunities have we got to develop and engage our people?	
		What are the threats with regard to skills shortages and retention of key people?	
What are the main strategic issues facing the business?		To what extent do these issues involve HR considerations?	
What are the drivers of performance in the business?		What contribution should our people make to drive performance?	

Tool 2 Analysis of competitive strategy and its implications

Strategy	HR Area	Possible Actions	Proposed Actions
Achieve competitive advantage through innovation	Resourcing	Recruit and retain high-quality people with innovative skills and a good track record in innovation.	
	Learning and development	Develop strategic capability and provide encouragement and facilities for enhancing innovative skills and enhancing the intellectual capital of the organization.	
	Reward	Provide financial incentives and rewards and recognition for successful innovations.	
Achieve competitive advantage through quality	Resourcing	Use sophisticated selection procedures to recruit people who are likely to deliver quality and high levels of customer service.	
	Learning and development	Encourage the development of a learning organization, develop and implement knowledge management processes, and support total quality and customer care initiatives with focused training.	
	Reward	Link rewards to quality performance and the achievement of high standards of customer service.	
Achieve competitive advantage through cost leadership	Resourcing	Develop core and periphery employment structures; recruit people who are likely to add value; if unavoidable, plan and manage downsizing humanely.	
	Learning and development	Provide training designed to improve productivity; inaugurate just-in-time training that is closely linked to immediate business needs and can generate measurable improvements in cost-effectiveness.	
	Reward	Develop performance management processes that enable both financial and non-financial rewards to be related to competence and skills; ensure that pay levels are competitive.	

Tool 3 Analysis of business strategies and their implications

Business Strategy		HR Implications			
		Performance	Resourcing	Learning and Development	Reward
Market Development					
Product Development					
New Technology					
Diversification					
Merger, Acquisition					

Tool 4 Analysis of fit between type of organization and HR strategy

Miles and Snow Classification	Implications for HR Strategy			
	Performance	Resourcing	Learning and Development	Reward
Prospectors, which operate in an environment characterized by rapid and unpredictable changes.				
Defenders, which operate in a more stable and predictable environment than prospectors and engage in more long-term planning.				
Analysers, which are a combination of the prospector and defender types. They operate in stable environments like defenders and also in markets where new products are constantly required like prospectors.				
Reactors, which are unstable organizations existing in what they believe to be an unpredictable environment. They lack consistent, well-articulated strategies and do not undertake long-range planning.				

Tool 5 'Best-practice' analysis

Pfeffer's List of Seven 'Best Practices'	'Best Practice' Adopted by Similar Organizations	Extent to which 'Best Practice' Exists in Own Organization	Extent to which 'Best Practice' Should or Can Be Adopted in Context of Own Organization
1. Employment security			
2. Selective hiring			
3. Self-managed teams			
4. High compensation contingent on performance			
5. Training to provide a skilled and motivated workforce			
6. Reduction of status differentials			
7. Sharing information			

Tool 6 Overall analysis of HR strategic goals

Possible HR Strategic Goals	Importance*	Effectiveness*
Support the achievement of the organization's goals		
Meet needs of employees		
Develop a high-performance culture		
Create a powerful employee value proposition		
Ensure that the organization is seen as a 'great place to work'		
Increase engagement		
Recruit and retain talented people		
Reward people according to their contribution		
Provide employees with a voice		
Improve communications		
Provide a good working environment		

* Scale: 10 = high; 0 = low

Tool 7 Overall strategic HRM gap analysis

Strategic HRM Area	What We Are Doing	What We Should Be Doing	How We Should Fill the Gap
Performance			
Engagement			
Organization Development			
Resourcing			
Talent Management			
Learning and Development			
Reward Management			
Employee Relations			
Working Environment			

Tool 8 Integration of business and HR strategies

Business Strategy	Integrated HR Strategy
1.	
2.	
3.	
4.	
5.	
6.	

Tool 9 Bundling of HR activities

Possible Areas in which Bundling (ie Linking HR Activities) Could Take Place	Extent to which Any Bundling Has Taken Place	Any Further Action Required
High-performance work system		
Performance management		
Use of competency framework		
Development of joined-up talent management processes		
Development of blended learning processes		
Development of career grade and pay structures		

Tool 10   Analysis of high-performance goals

Characteristics of the Culture	Importance*	Effectiveness*
People know what's expected of them – they understand their goals and accountabilities.		
People feel that their job is worth doing, and there is a strong fit between the job and their capabilities.		
Management defines what it requires in the shape of performance improvements, sets goals for success and monitors performance to ensure that the goals are achieved.		
There is strong leadership from the top that engenders a shared belief in the importance of continuing improvement.		
There is a focus on promoting positive attitudes that result in an engaged, committed and motivated workforce.		
Performance management processes are aligned to business goals to ensure that people are engaged in achieving agreed objectives and standards.		
Capacities of people are developed through learning at all levels to support performance improvement and are provided with opportunities to make full use of their skills and abilities.		
People are valued and rewarded according to their contribution.		
A pool of talent ensures a continuous supply of high performers in key roles.		
There is a climate of trust and teamwork, aimed at delivering a distinctive service to the customer.		

Scale: 10 = high; 0 = low

Tool 11 High-performance work system gap analysis

Strategic HPWS Area	What We Are Doing	What We Should Be Doing	How We Should Fill the Gap
Performance drivers identified and govern development of HPWS practices.			
Corporate performance goals cascaded to all employees.			
Roles clarify and emphasize performance goals.			
Effective performance management system in place.			
Rewards related to performance and contribution.			
Learning and development activities focus on delivering performance improvements.			
Performance improvement recognized as key aspect of leadership.			

Tool 12   Analysis of engagement and commitment levels – survey

Please circle the number that most closely matches your opinion.

	Strongly Agree	Disagree	Strongly Agree	Disagree
Engagement:				
1. I am very satisfied with the work I do.	1	2	3	4
2. My job is interesting.	1	2	3	4
3. I know exactly what I am expected to do.	1	2	3	4
4. I am prepared to put myself out to do my work.	1	2	3	4
5. My job is not very challenging.	1	2	3	4
6. I am given plenty of freedom to decide how to do my work.	1	2	3	4
7. I get plenty of opportunities to learn in this job.	1	2	3	4
8. The facilities / equipment / tools provided are excellent.	1	2	3	4
9. I do not get adequate support from my boss.	1	2	3	4
10. My contribution is fully recognized.	1	2	3	4
11. The experience I am getting now will be a great help in advancing my future career.	1	2	3	4
12. I find it difficult to keep up with the demands of my job.	1	2	3	4
13. I have no problems in achieving a balance between my work and my private life.	1	2	3	4
14. I like working for my boss.	1	2	3	4
15. I get on well with my work colleagues.	1	2	3	4
Commitment:				
16. I think this organization is a great place in which to work.	1	2	3	4
17. I believe I have a good future in this organization.	1	2	3	4
18. I intend to go on working for this organization.	1	2	3	4
19. I am not happy about the values of this organization – the ways in which it conducts its business.	1	2	3	4
20. I believe that the products / services provided by this organization are excellent.	1	2	3	4

Tool 13 Analysis of employee engagement goals

Engagement Goals – Enhance Engagement by:	Importance*	Effectiveness*
Providing interesting and challenging work, responsibility (feeling that the work is important and having control over one's own resources), autonomy (freedom to act), scope to use and develop skills and abilities, the availability of the resources required to carry out the work, and opportunities for advancement.		
Establishing an enabling, supportive and inspirational work environment.		
Ensuring that leaders increase engagement through the ways in which they design jobs, allocate work, delegate and provide autonomy.		
Providing people with opportunities to grow and develop.		
Enabling people to feed their ideas and views upwards and feel they are making a contribution.		

* Scale: 10 = high; 0 = low

Tool 14 Employee engagement gap analysis

Engagement Activity	What We Are Doing	What We Should Be Doing	How We Should Fill the Gap
Job Design			
Performance Management			
Total Reward System			
Leadership Development			
Skills and Career Development Opportunities			

Tool 15   Analysis of resourcing goals

Resourcing Goals	Importance*	Effectiveness*
Match people resources to business requirements.		
Avoid unexpected deficits or surpluses of staff.		
Achieve human capital advantage by employing higher-quality people than competitors.		
Attract and recruit high-quality candidates.		
Minimize recruitment costs.		
Maximize 'recruitment intensity', ie high numbers of applicants per vacancy.		
Increase predictive validity, ie the extent to which predictions of performance and overall suitability made when recruiting people are achieved.		
Increase retention rates.		
Reduce cost of labour turnover.		
Achieve the required degree of flexibility in the use of people.		

* Scale: 10 = high; 0 = low

Tool 16 Resourcing gap analysis

Resourcing Activity	What We Are Doing	What We Should Be Doing	How We Should Fill the Gap
Workforce planning based on thorough analysis of demand and supply forecasts.			
Take action to align resourcing plans to strategic business plans.			
Attractive employment brand developed to obtain good candidates.			
Speedy action taken to deal with forecast surpluses or deficits of staff.			
Use of a variety of potentially valuable sources of candidates.			
Role analysis uses competency framework and forms basis for structured interviews.			
Line managers trained in interviewing techniques.			
Interviews supplemented by batteries of valid and reliable tests.			
Causes of labour turnover analysed and action taken to reduce losses.			
Costs of labour turnover known and used to deliver message on the need to improve retention rates.			
Risk analysis carried out to identify potential losses and take preventative action.			
Effectiveness of resourcing activities regularly reviewed and corrective action taken as necessary.			

Tool 17   Analysis of talent management goals

Talent Management Goals	Importance*	Effectiveness*
Define what is meant by talent in terms of competencies and potential.		
Ensure that talent is treated as a key corporate resource.		
Develop a pool of talent that will provide a guaranteed supply of high-quality people to meet future requirements.		
Provide for management succession.		
Rely primarily on growth from within while recognizing the need to bring in fresh blood from time to time.		
Identify those with talent and potential.		
Institute programmes to develop talent.		
Create a compelling 'employee value proposition'.		
Develop the organization as 'an employer of choice'.		

* Scale: 10 = high; 0 = low

Tool 18   Talent management gap analysis

Talent Management Activity	What We Are Doing	What We Should Be Doing	How We Should Fill the Gap
Define organization's talent requirements.			
Conduct talent audits to identify talent.			
Identify sources of talent from within and outside the organization.			
Provide talented people with opportunities for career development and growth.			
Design jobs that provide talented people with the opportunity to develop their skills and potential.			
Define career paths and career 'aiming points' or 'destination jobs'.			
Apply systematic policies to improve retention rates.			
Create management succession plans.			
Recognize those with talent through the reward system.			

Tool 19 Analysis of learning and development goals

Learning and Development Goals	Importance*	Effectiveness*
Create human capital advantage by ensuring that the organization has more skilled and competent people than its competitors.		
Improve individual, team and organizational performance.		
Attract and retain high-quality people by offering them learning and development opportunities.		
Extend the skills base of the organization.		
Improve organizational flexibility by multiskilling.		
Provide additional non-financial rewards to people in the form of growth and career opportunities.		
Reduce the length of learning curves and thus minimize learning costs.		
Ensure that talented people are developed to achieve their maximum potential.		
Provide line managers with the skills required to lead and develop their people.		

* Scale: 10 = high; 0 = low

Tool 20   Gap analysis of learning and development activities

Learning and Development Activity	What We Are Doing	What We Should Be Doing	How We Should Fill the Gap
Encourage organizational learning.			
Develop the business as a learning organization.			
Identify learning needs.			
Introduce blended learning and development programmes to meet identified needs.			
Make good use of e-learning.			
Introduce systematic coaching.			
Develop a mentoring programme.			
Evaluate the outcome of learning and development programmes.			

Tool 21 Analysis of reward management goals

Reward Management Goals	Importance*	Effectiveness*
Reinforce the achievement of organizational goals.		
Recruit and retain staff of the required calibre.		
Facilitate staff mobility.		
Achieve strong relationship between pay and performance.		
Reinforce organizational values.		
Engage and motivate employees.		
Cost-effective.		
Well communicated and understood by employees.		
Managed effectively in practice by line managers.		

* Scale: 10 = high; 0 = low

Tool 22 Gap analysis of reward management activities

Reward Management Activity	What We Are Doing	What We Should Be Doing	How We Should Fill the Gap
Develop total reward processes.			
Use systematic processes for valuing roles and achieving internal equity.			
Regularly survey market rates to ensure pay levels are competitive.			
Develop and maintain grade and pay structures that provide a good framework for managing gradings and pay progression.			
Reward people for their contribution.			
Develop recognition programmes.			
Introduce flexible benefits.			
Manage general and individual pay reviews.			

Tool 23 Analysis of employee relations goals

Employee Relations Goals	Importance*	Effectiveness*
Build stable and cooperative relationships with employees and their trade unions.		
Operate on a partnership basis with trade unions.		
Achieve engagement through employee involvement and communication processes.		
Minimize conflict with employees and their unions.		
Adopt a high-commitment approach that develops mutuality.		
Maintain bargaining structures and negotiating procedures that enable agreements to be reached smoothly.		

* Scale: 10 = high; 0 = low

Tool 24 Gap analysis of employee relations activities

Employee Relations Activity	What We Are Doing	What We Should Be Doing	How We Should Fill the Gap
Recognize unions.			
Develop partnership agreements.			
Maintain effective industrial relations procedures.			
Resolve disputes.			
Negotiate terms and conditions.			
Communicate.			
Provide employees with a voice (involvement and participation).			

References

Abell, D F (1993) *Managing with Dual Strategies: Mastering the present, pre-empting the future*, Free Press, New York

Accounting for People Task Force (2003) *Accounting for People*, Department of Trade and Industry, London

Alderfer, C (1972) *Existence, Relatedness and Growth*, Free Press, New York

Allen, M R and White, P (2007) Strategic management and HRM, in *Oxford Handbook of Human Resource Management*, ed Peter Boxall, John Purcell and Patrick Wright, Oxford University Press, Oxford

Andrews, K A (1987) *The Concept of Corporate Strategy*, Irwin, Georgetown, Ontario

Ansoff, H I (1987) *Corporate Strategy*, McGraw-Hill, New York

Appelbaum, E, Bailey, T, Berg, P and Kalleberg, A L (2000) *Manufacturing Advantage: Why high performance work systems pay off*, ILR Press, Ithaca, NY

Argyris, C (1970) *Intervention Theory and Method*, Addison-Wesley, Reading, MA

Argyris, L (1992) *On Organizational Learning*, Jossey-Bass, San Francisco

Armitage, A and Keeble-Allen, D (2007) Why people management basics form the foundation of high-performance working, *People Management*, 18 October, p 48

Armstrong, M (2000) The name has changed but has the game remained the same?, *Employee Relations*, **22** (6), pp 576–89

Armstrong, M and Baron, A (2002) *Strategic HRM: The route to improved business performance*, CIPD, London

Armstrong, M and Brown, D (2007) *Strategic Reward*, Kogan Page, London

Armstrong, M and Long, P (1994) *The Reality of Strategic HRM*, Institute of Personnel and Development, London

Arthur, J (1990) Industrial relations and business strategies in American steel minimills, Unpublished PhD dissertation, Cornell University, Ithaca, NY

Arthur, J B (1992) The link between business strategy and industrial relations systems in American steel mills, *Industrial and Labor Relations Review*, **45** (3), pp 488–506

Arthur, J (1994) Effects of human resource systems on manufacturing performance and turnover, *Academy of Management Review*, **37** (4), pp 670–87

Ashton, D and Sung, J (2002) *Supporting Workplace Learning for High Performance*, International Labour Organization, Geneva

Atkinson, J (1984) Manpower strategies for flexible organizations, *Personnel Management*, August, pp 28–31

Baird, L and Meshoulam, I (1988) Managing two fits of strategic human resource management, *Academy of Management Review*, **13** (1), pp 116–28

Bandura, A (1977) *Social Learning Theory*, Prentice-Hall, Englewood Cliffs, NJ

Barney, J B (1991) Firm resources and sustained competitive advantage, *Journal of Management Studies*, **17** (1), pp 99–120

Barney, J B (1995) Looking inside for competitive advantage, *Academy of Management Executive*, **9** (4), pp 49–61

Baron, D (2001) Private policies, corporate policies and integrated strategy, *Journal of Economics and Management Strategy*, **10** (7), pp 7–45

Baron, R and Kreps, D (1999) *Strategic Human Resources: Frameworks for general managers*, Wiley, New York

Bass, B M and Vaughan, J A (1966) *Training in Industry: The management of learning*, Tavistock, London

Batt, R (2007) Service strategies, in *Oxford Handbook of Human Resource Management*, ed Peter Boxall, John Purcell and Patrick Wright, Oxford University Press, Oxford

Becker, B E and Gerhart, B (1996) The impact of human resource management on organisational performance, progress and prospects, *Academy of Management Journal*, **39** (4), pp 779–801

Becker, B E and Huselid, M A (1998) High performance work systems and firm performance: a synthesis of research and managerial implications, *Research on Personnel and Human Resource Management*, **16**, pp 53–101, JAI Press, Stamford, CT

Becker, B E, Huselid, M A, Pickus, P S and Spratt, M F (1997) HR as a source of shareholder value: research and recommendations, *Human Resource Management*, Spring, **36** (1), pp 39–47

Becker, B E, Huselid, M A and Ulrich, D (2001) *The HR Score Card: Linking people, strategy, and performance*, Harvard Business School Press, Boston, MA

Beckhard, R (1989) A model for the executive management of transformational change, in *Human Resource Strategies*, ed G Salaman, Sage, London

Beer, M (1980) *Organization Change and Development: A systems view*, Goodyear, Santa Monica, CA

Beer, M, Spector, B, Lawrence, P, Quinn Mills, D and Walton, R (1984) *Managing Human Assets*, Free Press, New York

Benson, G S, Young, S M and Lawler, E E (2006) High involvement work practices and analysts' forecasts of corporate performance, *Human Resource Management*, **45** (4), pp 519–27

Bevan, S, Barber, L and Robinson, D (1997) *Keeping the Best: A practical guide to retaining key employees*, Institute for Employment Studies, Brighton

Blackler, F (1995) Knowledge, knowledge work and experience, *Organization Studies*, **16** (6), pp 16–36

Blake, P (1988) The knowledge management explosion, *Information Today*, **15** (1), pp 12–13

Blake, R, Shepart, H and Mouton, J (1964) Breakthrough in organizational development, *Harvard Business Review*, **42**, pp 237–58

Bontis, N, Dragonetti, N C, Jacobsen, K and Roos, G (1999) The knowledge toolbox: a review of the tools available to measure and manage intangible resources, *European Management Journal*, **17** (4), pp 391–402

Bower, J L (1982) Business policy in the 1980s, *Academy of Management Review*, **7** (4), pp 630–38

Boxall, P F (1992) Strategic HRM: a beginning, a new theoretical direction, *Human Resource Management Journal*, **2** (3), pp 61–79

Boxall, P F (1993) The significance of human resource management: a reconsideration of the evidence, *International Journal of Human Resource Management*, **4** (3), pp 645–65

Boxall, P F (1996) The strategic HRM debate and the resource-based view of the firm, *Human Resource Management Journal*, **6** (3), pp 59–75

Boxall, P F and Purcell, J (2003) *Strategy and Human Resource Management*, Palgrave Macmillan, Basingstoke

Boxall, P F, Purcell, J and Wright, P (2007) Human resource management: scope, analysis and significance, in *Oxford Handbook of Human Resource Management*, ed Peter Boxall, John Purcell and Patrick Wright, Oxford University Press, Oxford

Brown, D (2001) *Reward Strategies: From intent to impact*, Chartered Institute of Personnel and Development, London

Bulla, D N and Scott, P M (1994) Manpower requirements forecasting: a case example, in *Human Resource Forecasting and Modelling*, ed D Ward, T P Bechet and R Tripp, Human Resource Planning Society, New York

Buller, P F and Napier, N K (1993) Strategy and human resource management: integration in fast growth versus other mid-sized firms, *British Journal of Management*, **4** (1), pp 77–90

Burgoyne, J (1994) As reported in *Personnel Management Plus*, May, p 7

Burns, B (1992) *Managing Change*, Pitman, London

Burns, J M (1978) *Leadership*, Harper & Row, New York

Business in the Community (2007) *Benchmarking Responsible Business Practice*, www.bitc.org.uk

Butler, J E, Ferris, G R and Napier, N K (1991) *Strategy and Human Resource Management*, South-Western Publishing, Cincinnati, OH

Caldwell, R (2004) Rhetoric, facts and self-fulfilling prophesies: exploring practitioners' perceptions of progress in implementing HRM, *Industrial Relations Journal*, **35** (3), pp 196–215

Cappelli, P (1999) *Employment Practices and Business Strategy*, Oxford University Press, New York

Cappelli, P and Crocker-Hefter, A (1996) Distinctive human resources are firms' core competencies, *Organizational Dynamics*, Winter, pp 7–22

Chandler, A D (1962) *Strategy and Structure*, MIT Press, Boston, MA

Chartered Institute of Personnel and Development (CIPD) (2004) *Professional Standards*, http://www.cipd.co.uk

CIPD (2005) *Thinking Performer*, http://www.cipd.co.uk

CIPD (2007a) *HR Business Partnering*, CIPD, London

CIPD (2007b) *Talent Management Partnering*, CIPD, London

Chatzkel, J L (2004) Human capital: the rules of engagement are changing, *Lifelong Learning in Europe*, **9** (3), pp 139–45

Child, J (1972) Organizational structure, environment and performance: the role of strategic choice, *Sociology*, **6** (3), pp 1–22

Conference Board (2006) *Employee Engagement: A review of current research and its implications*, Conference Board, New York

Cowling, A and Walters, M (1990) Manpower planning: where are we today?, *Personnel Review*, March, pp 9–15

Cox, A and Purcell, J (1998) Searching for leverage: pay systems, trust, motivation and commitment in SMEs, in *Trust, Motivation and Commitment*, ed S J Perkins and St J Sandringham, Strategic Remuneration Centre, Faringdon

CSR Academy (2006) *The CSR Competency Framework*, Stationery Office, Norwich

Cummins, T G and Worley, C G (2005) *Organization Development and Change*, South-Western Publishing, Mason, OH

Davenport, T H (1996) Why re-engineering failed: the fad that forgot people, *Fast Company*, Premier issue, pp 70–74

Delery, J E and Doty, H D (1996) Modes of theorizing in strategic human resource management: tests of universality, contingency and configurational performance predictions, *Academy of Management Journal*, **39** (4), pp 802–35

Deming, W E (1986) *Out of the Crisis*, MIT Center for Advanced Engineering Study, Cambridge, MA

Department of Trade and Industry (DTI) and Department for Education and Employment (DfEE) (1997) *Partnerships at Work*, DTI and DfEE, London

Dickens, C (1843) *Martin Chuzzlewit*, Chapman & Hall, London

Digman, L A (1990) *Strategic Management: Concepts, decisions, cases*, Irwin, Georgetown, Ontario

Donkin, R (2005) *Human Capital Management: A management report*, Croner, London

Doty, D H, Glick, W H and Huber, G P (1993) Fit, equifinality, and organizational effectiveness: a test of two configurational theories, *Academy of Management Journal*, **36** (6), pp 1195–250

Drucker, P E (1955) *The Practice of Management*, Heinemann, London

Dyer, L and Holder, G W (1988) Strategic human resource management and planning, in *Human Resource Management: Evolving roles and responsibilities*, ed L Dyer, Bureau of National Affairs, Washington, DC

Dyer, L and Reeves, T (1995) Human resource strategies and firm performance: what do we know and where do we need to go?, *International Journal of Human Resource Management*, **6** (3), pp 656–70

Egan, J (2006) Doing the decent thing: CSR and ethics in employment, *IRS Employment Review*, **858**, 3 November, pp 9–16

Ehrenberg, R G and Smith, R S (1994) *Modern Labor Economics*, HarperCollins, New York

Ericksen, J (2007) High performance work systems: dynamic workforce alignment and firm performance, *Academy of Management Proceedings*, pp 1–6

Faulkner, D and Johnson, G (1992) *The Challenge of Strategic Management*, Kogan Page, London

Fombrun, C J, Tichy, N M and Devanna, M A (1984) *Strategic Human Resource Management*, Wiley, New York

Fowler, A (1987) When chief executives discover HRM, *Personnel Management*, January, p 3

Francis, H and Keegan, A (2006) The changing face of HRM: in search of balance, *Human Resource Management Journal*, **16** (3), pp 231–49

Freeman, R E (1984) *Strategic Management: A stakeholder perspective*, Prentice-Hall, Englewood Cliffs, NJ

French, W L and Bell, C H (1990) *Organization Development*, Prentice-Hall, Englewood Cliffs, NJ

French, W L, Kast, F E and Rosenzweig, J E (1985) *Understanding Human Behaviour in Organizations*, Harper & Row, New York

Friedman, M (1970) The social responsibility of business is to increase its profits, *New York Times Magazine*, September, p 13

Garvin, D A (1993) Building a learning organization, *Harvard Business Review*, July–August, pp 78–91

Gephart, M A (1995) The road to high performance: steps to create a high-performance workplace, *Training and Development*, June, p 29

Goold, M and Campbell, A (1986) *Strategies and Styles: The role of the centre in managing diversified corporations*, Blackwell, Oxford

Grant, R M (1991) The resource-based theory of competitive advantage: implications for strategy formulation, *California Management Review*, **33** (3), pp 114–35

Gratton, L (1999) People processes as a source of competitive advantage, in *Strategic Human Resource Management*, ed L Gratton *et al*, Oxford University Press, Oxford

Gratton, L A (2000) Real step change, *People Management*, 16 March, pp 27–30

Gratton, L, Hailey, V, Stiles, P and Truss, C (1999) *Strategic Human Resource Management*, Oxford University Press, Oxford

Guest, D E (1987) Human resource management and industrial relations, *Journal of Management Studies*, **14** (5), pp 503–21

Guest, D E (1989a) Human resource management: its implications for industrial relations and trade unions, in *New Perspectives in Human Resource Management*, ed J Storey, Routledge, London

Guest, D E (1989b) Personnel and HRM: can you tell the difference?, *Personnel Management*, January, pp 48–51

Guest, D E (1991) Personnel management: the end of orthodoxy, *British Journal of Industrial Relations*, **29** (2), pp 149–76

Guest, D E (1995) Human resource management: trade unions and industrial relations, in *Human Resource Management: A critical text*, ed J Storey, Routledge, London

Guest, D E (1997) Human resource management and performance: a review of the research agenda, *International Journal of Human Resource Management*, **8** (3), pp 263–76

Guest, D E (1999) Human resource management: the workers' verdict, *Human Resource Management Journal*, **9** (2), pp 5–25

Guest, D E and Conway, N (1997) *Employee Motivation and the Psychological Contract*, Institute of Personnel and Development, London

Guest, D E, Michie, J, Sheehan, M and Conway, N (2000a) *Employee Relations, HRM and Business Performance: An analysis of the 1998 Workplace Employee Relations Survey*, Chartered Institute of Personnel and Development, London

Guest, D E, Michie, J, Sheehan, M and Conway, N (2000b) *Effective People Management: Initial findings of Future of Work Survey*, Chartered Institute of Personnel and Development, London

Guest, D E, Michie, J, Sheehan, M, Conway, N and Shehan, M (2003) Human resource management and corporate performance in the UK, *British Journal of Industrial Relations*, **41** (2), pp 291–314

Hamel, G and Prahalad, C K (1989) Strategic intent, *Harvard Business Review*, May–June, pp 63–76

Hansen, M T, Nohria, N and Tierney, T (1999) What's your strategy for managing knowledge?, *Harvard Business Review*, March–April, pp 106–16

Harrison, R (1997) *Employee Development*, 2nd edn, Institute of Personnel and Development, London

Harrison, R (2000) *Employee Development*, 3rd edn, Chartered Institute of Personnel and Development, London

Heller, R (1972) *The Naked Manager*, Barrie & Jenkins, London

Hendry, C and Pettigrew, A (1986) The practice of strategic human resource management, *Personnel Review*, **15**, pp 2–8

Hendry, C and Pettigrew, A (1990) Human resource management: an agenda for the 1990s, *International Journal of Human Resource Management*, **1** (3), pp 17–43

Hillman, A and Keim, G (2001) Shareholder value, stakeholder management and social issues: what's the bottom line?, *Strategic Management Journal*, **22** (2), pp 125–39

Hofer, C W and Schendel, D (1986) *Strategy Formulation: Analytical concepts*, West Publishing, New York

Huselid, M A (1995) The impact of human resource management practices on turnover, productivity and corporate financial performance, *Academy of Management Journal*, **38** (3), pp 635–72

Huselid, M A and Becker, B E (1996) Methodological issues in cross-sectional and panel estimates of the human resource–firm performance link, *Industrial Relations*, **35** (3), pp 400–22

Husted, B W and Salazar, J (2006) Taking Friedman seriously: maximizing profits and social performance, *Journal of Management Studies*, **43** (1), pp 75–91

Incomes Data Services (IDS) (2007) Building an engaged workforce, *HR Studies Update*, May, pp 1–3

Industrial Relations Services (IRS) (1993) Multi-employer bargaining, *IRS Employment Trends*, **544**, pp 6–8

Johnson, G and Scholes, K (1993) *Exploring Corporate Strategy*, Prentice Hall, Hemel Hempstead

Kamoche, K (1996) Strategic human resource management within a resource capability view of the firm, *Journal of Management Studies*, **33** (2), pp 213–33

Kant, I (2003 [1781]) *Critique of Pure Reason*, Dover Publications, Mineola, NY

Kanter, R M (1984) *The Change Masters*, Allen & Unwin, London

Kay, J (1999) Strategy and the illusions of grand designs, Mastering Strategy, *Financial Times*, 21 May, pp 2–4

Kearns, P (2005) *Human Capital Management*, Reed Business Information, Sutton, Surrey

Keenoy, T (1990a) HRM: a case of the wolf in sheep's clothing, *Personnel Review*, **19** (2), pp 3–9

Keenoy, T (1997) HRMism and the images of re-presentation, *Journal of Management Studies*, **4** (5), pp 825–41

Keep, E (1989) Corporate training strategies, in *New Perspectives on Human Resource Management*, ed J Storey, Blackwell, Oxford

King, J (1995) High performance work systems and firm performance, *Monthly Labour Review*, May, pp 29–36

Kochan, T A (2007) Social legitimacy of the HR profession, in *Oxford Handbook of Human Resource Management*, ed Peter Boxall, John Purcell and Patrick Wright, Oxford University Press, Oxford

Kochan, T, Katz, H and McKersie, R (1986) *The Transformation of American Industrial Relations*, Basic Books, New York

Kolb, D A (1984) *Experiential Learning: Experience as the source of learning and development*, Prentice-Hall, Englewood Cliffs, NJ

Kotter, J J (1995) *A 20% Solution: Using rapid re-design to build tomorrow's organization today*, Wiley, New York

Lawler, E E (1969) Job design and employee motivation, *Personnel Psychology*, **22**, pp 426–35

Lawler, E E (1986) *High Involvement Management*, Jossey-Bass, San Francisco

Lawler, E E (2003) *Treat People Right! How organizations and individuals can propel each other into a virtuous spiral of success*, Jossey-Bass, San Francisco

Lawler, E E, Mohrman, S and Ledford, G (1998) *Strategies for High Performance Organizations: Employee involvement, TQM, and re-engineering programs in Fortune 1000*, Jossey-Bass, San Francisco

Legge, K (1989) Human resource management: a critical analysis, in *New Perspectives in Human Resource Management*, ed J Storey, Routledge, London

Legge, K (1995) *Human Resource Management: Rhetorics and realities*, Macmillan, London

Legge, K (1998) The morality of HRM, in *Experiencing Human Resource Management*, ed C Mabey, D Skinner and T Clark, Sage, London

Lengnick-Hall, C A and Lengnick-Hall, M L (1988) Review of the literature and proposed typology, *Academy of Management Review*, **13** (3), pp 454–70

Lengnick-Hall, C A and Lengnick-Hall, M L (1990) *Interactive Human Resource Management and Strategic Planning*, Quorum Books, Westport, CT

Levitt, T (1958) The dangers of social responsibility, *Harvard Business Review*, September–October, pp 41–50

Lewin, K (1947) Frontiers in group dynamics, *Human Relations*, **1** (1), pp 5–42

Lewin, K (1951) *Field Theory in Social Science*, Harper & Row, New York

Mabey, C, Skinner, D and Clark, T (1998) *Experiencing Human Resource Management*, Sage, London

MacDuffie, J P (1995) Human resource bundles and manufacturing performance, *Industrial Relations Review*, **48** (2), pp 199–221

Manocha, R (2005) Grand totals, *People Management*, 7 April, pp 27–31

Marchington, M and Wilkinson, A (1996) *Core Personnel and Development*, Institute of Personnel and Development, London

Marchington, M, Wilkinson, A, Ackers, P and Dundon, A (2001) *Management Choice and Employee Voice*, Chartered Institute of Personnel and Development, London

Marsick, V J (1994) Trends in managerial invention: creating a learning map, *Management Learning*, 21 (1), pp 11–33

McGregor, D (1960) *The Human Side of Enterprise*, McGraw-Hill, New York

McWilliams, A and Siegel, D S (2000) Corporate social responsibility and financial performance: correlation or misspecification?, *Strategic Management Journal*, **21** (5), pp 603–09

McWilliams, A, Siegel, D S and Wright, P M (2006) Corporate social responsibility: strategic implications, *Journal of Management Studies*, **43** (1), pp 1–12

Mecklenberg, S, Deering, A and Sharp, D (1999) Knowledge management: a secret engine of corporate growth, *Executive Agenda*, **2**, pp 5–15

Meyer, A D, Tsui, A S and Hinings, C R (1993) Configurational approaches to organizational analysis, *Academy of Management Journal*, **36** (6), pp 1175–95

Michaels, E, Handfield-Jones, H and Axelrod, B (2001) *The War for Talent*, Harvard Business School Press, Boston, MA

Miles, R E and Snow, C C (1978) *Organizational Strategy: Structure and process*, McGraw-Hill, New York

Miller, A and Dess, G G (1996) *Strategic Management*, 2nd edn, McGraw-Hill, New York

Miller, S, Hickson, D J and Wilson, D C (1999) Decision-making in organizations, in *Managing Organizations: Current issues*, ed S R Clegg, C Hardy and W R Nord, Sage, London

Millward, N, Bryson, A and Forth, J (2000) *All Change at Work: British employment relations as portrayed by the Workshop Industrial Relations Survey Series*, Routledge, London

Mintzberg, H T (1978) Patterns in strategy formation, *Management Science*, May, pp 934–48

Mintzberg, H T (1979) *The Structuring of Organizations*, Prentice-Hall, Englewood Cliffs, NJ

Mintzberg, H T (1987) Crafting strategy, *Harvard Business Review*, July–August, pp 66–74

Mintzberg, H T (1994) The rise and fall of strategic planning, *Harvard Business Review*, January–February, pp 107–14

Mintzberg, H, Quinn, J B and James, R M (1988) *The Strategy Process: Concepts, contexts and cases*, Prentice-Hall, New York

Moore, J I (1992) *Writers on Strategic Management*, Penguin Books, London

Moran, P and Ghoshal, S (1996) Value creation by firms, Best Paper Proceedings, Academy of Management Annual Meeting, Cincinnati, OH

Murlis, H (1996) *Pay at the Crossroads*, Institute of Personnel and Development, London

Nadler, D A (1989) Organizational architecture for the corporation of the future, *Benchmark*, Fall, pp 12–13

Nadler, D A and Gerstein, M S (1992) Designing high-performance work systems: organizing people, technology, work and information, *Organizational Architecture*, Summer, pp 195–208

Nahapiet, J and Ghoshal, S (1998) Social capital, intellectual capital and the organizational advantage, *Academy of Management Review*, **23** (2), pp 242–66

Nalbantian, R, Guzzo, R A, Kieffer, D and Doherty, J (2004) *Play to Your Strengths: Managing your internal labor markets for lasting competitive advantage*, McGraw-Hill, New York

Nonaka, I (1991) The knowledge creating company, *Harvard Business Review*, November–December, pp 96–104

Nonaka, I and Takeuchi, H (1995) *The Knowledge Creating Company*, Oxford University Press, New York

Noon, M (1992) HRM: a map, model or theory?, in *Reassessing Human Resource Management*, ed P Blyton and P Turnbull, Sage, London

Ondrack, D A and Nininger, J R (1984) Human resource strategies: the corporate perspective, *Business Quarterly*, **49** (4), pp 101–09

Paauwe, J (2004) *HRM and Performance*, Oxford University Press, Oxford

Pascale, R (1990) *Managing on the Edge*, Viking, London

Patterson, M G, West, M A, Lawthom, R and Nickell, S (1997) *Impact of People Management Practices on Performance*, Institute of Personnel and Development, London

Pearce, J A and Robinson, R B (1988) *Strategic Management: Strategy formulation and implementation*, Irwin, Georgetown, Ontario

Pedler, M, Boydell, T and Burgoyne, J (1989) Towards the learning company, *Management Education and Development*, **20** (1), pp 1–8

Penrose, E (1959) *The Theory of the Growth of the Firm*, Blackwell, Oxford

Pettigrew, A and Whipp, R (1991) *Managing Change for Strategic Success*, Blackwell, Oxford

Pfeffer, J (1994) *Competitive Advantage through People*, Harvard Business School Press, Boston, MA

Pfeffer, J (2001) Fighting the war for talent is hazardous to your organization's health, *Organization Dynamics*, **29** (4), pp 248–59

Pickard, J (2005) Part not partner, *People Management*, 27 October, pp 48–50

Pil, F K and MacDuffie, J P (1996) The adoption of high-involvement work practices, *Industrial Relations*, **35** (3), pp 423–55

Porter, M E (1985) *Competitive Advantage: Creating and sustaining superior performance*, Free Press, New York

Porter, M E and Kramer, M R (2006) Strategy and society: the link between competitive advantage and corporate social responsibility, *Harvard Business Review*, December, pp 78–92

Prahalad, C K and Hamel, G (1990) The core competences of the organization, *Harvard Business Review*, May–June, pp 79–93

Purcell, J (1989) The impact of corporate strategy on human resource management, in *New Perspectives on Human Resource Management*, ed J Storey, Routledge, London

Purcell, J (1993) The challenge of human resource management for industrial relations research and practice, *International Journal of Human Resource Management*, **4** (3), pp 511–27

Purcell, J (1999) Best practice or best fit: chimera or cul-de-sac?, *Human Resource Management Journal*, **9** (3), pp 26–41

Purcell, J (2001) The meaning of strategy in human resource management, in *Human Resource Management: A critical text*, ed J Storey, Thomson Learning, London

Purcell, J and Ahlstrand, B (1994) *Human Resource Management in the Multidivisional Company*, Oxford University Press, Oxford

Purcell, J, Kinnie, K, Hutchinson, S, Rayton, B and Swart, J (2003) *Understanding the People and Performance Link: Unlocking the black box*, Chartered Institute of Personnel and Development, London

Quinn, J B (1980) *Strategies for Change: Logical incrementalism*, Irwin, Georgetown, Ontario

Quinn Mills, D (1983) Planning with people in mind, *Harvard Business Review*, November–December, pp 97–105

Ramsay, H, Scholarios, D and Harley, B (2000) Employees and high-performance work systems: testing inside the black box, *British Journal of Industrial Relations*, **38** (4), pp 501–31

Ready, D A and Conger, J A (2007) Make your company a talent factory, *Harvard Business Review*, June, pp 68–77

Redington, I (2005) *Making CSR Happen: The contribution of people management*, Chartered Institute of Personnel and Development, London

Reynolds, J (2004) *Helping People Learn*, Chartered Institute of Personnel and Development, London

Reynolds, J, Caley, L and Mason, R (2002) *How Do People Learn?*, Chartered Institute of Personnel and Development, London

Richardson, R and Thompson, M (1999) *The Impact of People Management Practices on Business Performance: A literature review*, Institute of Personnel and Development, London

Robinson, D, Perryman, S and Hayday, S (2004) *The Drivers of Employee Engagement*, Institute of Employment Studies, Brighton

Roscow, J and Casner-Lotto, J (1998) *People, Partnership and Profits: The new labor-management agenda*, Work in America Institute, New York

Rothwell, S (1995) Human resource planning, in *Human Resource Management: A critical text*, ed J Storey, Routledge, London

Rumelt, R P (1984) Towards a strategic theory of the firm, in *Competitive Strategic Management*, ed P C Nystrom and W H Starbuck, Prentice-Hall, Englewood Cliffs, NJ

Russo, M V and Fouts, P A (1997) A resource-based perspective on corporate environmental performance and profitability, *Academy of Management Review*, **40** (3), pp 534–59

Scarborough, H and Elias, J (2002) *Evaluating Human Capital*, Chartered Institute of Personnel and Development, London

Scarborough, H, Swan, J and Preston, J (1999) *Knowledge Management: A literature review*, Institute of Personnel and Development, London

Schein, E H (1969) *Process Consultation: Its role in organizational development*, Addison-Wesley, Reading, MA

Schein, E H (1990) Organizational culture, *American Psychologist*, **45**, pp 109–19

Schuler, R S (1992) Strategic human resource management: linking people with the strategic needs of the business, *Organizational Dynamics*, **21** (1), pp 18–32

Schuler, R S and Jackson, S E (1987) Linking competitive strategies with human resource management practices, *Academy of Management Executive*, **9** (3), pp 207–19

Schuler, R S and Walker, J (1990) Human resources strategy: focusing on issues and actions, *Organization Dynamics*, Summer, pp 5–19

Scott, A (1994) *Willing Slaves? British workers under human resource management*, Cambridge University Press, Cambridge

Sears, D (2003) *Successful Talent Strategies*, American Management Association, New York

Senge, P (1990) *The Fifth Discipline: The art and practice of the learning organization*, Random Century, New York

Sisson, K (1990) Introducing the Human Resource Management Journal, *Human Resource Management Journal*, **1** (1), pp 1–11

Sloman, M (1999) Seize the day, *People Management*, 20 May, p 31

Sloman, M (2003) *Training in the Age of the Learner*, Chartered Institute of Personnel and Development, London

Smethurst, S (2005) The long and winding road, *People Management*, 28 July, pp 25–29

Smith, E C (1982) Strategic business planning and human resources, *Personnel Journal*, **61** (8), pp 606–10

Spellman, R (1992) Gaining a competitive advantage in the labour market, in *Strategies for Human Resource Management*, ed Michael Armstrong, Kogan Page, London

Stevens, J (2005) *High Performance Wales: Real experiences, real success*, Wales Management Council, Cardiff

Storey, J (1989) From personnel management to human resource management, in *New Perspectives on Human Resource Management*, ed J Storey, Routledge, London

Storey, J (1993) The take-up of human resource management by main-stream companies: key lessons from research, *International Journal of Human Resource Management*, **4** (3), pp 60–65

Sung, J and Ashton, D (2005) *High Performance Work Practices: Linking strategy and skills to performance outcomes*, DTI in association with CIPD, http://www.cipd.co.uk/subjects/corpstrtgy

Taylor, S (1998) *Employee Resourcing*, Institute of Personnel and Development, London

Teece, D, Pisano, G and Shuen, A (1997) Dynamic capabilities and strategic management, *Strategic Management Journal*, **18**, pp 509–33

Thompson, M (2002) *High Performance Work Organization in UK Aerospace*, Society of British Aerospace Companies, London

Thompson, M and Heron, P (2005) Management capability and high performance work organization, *International Journal of Human Resource Management*, **16** (6), pp 1029–48

Thompson, P and Harley, B (2007) HRM and the worker: labour process perspectives, in *Oxford Handbook of Human Resource Management*, ed Peter Boxall, John Purcell and Patrick Wright, Oxford University Press, Oxford

Thorne, K and Pellant, A (2007) *The Essential Guide to Managing Talent*, Kogan Page, London

Towers Perrin (2007) *Global Workforce Study*, http://www.towersperrin.com

Townley, B (1989) Selection and appraisal: reconstructing social relations?, in *New Perspectives in Human Resource Management*, ed J Storey, Routledge, London

Truss, C (1999) Soft and hard models of HRM, in *Strategic Human Resource Management*, ed L Gratton *et al*, Oxford University Press, Oxford

Trussler, S (1998) The rules of the game, *Journal of Business Strategy*, **19** (1), pp 16–19

Tushman, M, Newman, W and Nadler, D (1988) Executive leadership and organizational evolution: managing incremental and discontinuous change, in *Corporate Transformation: Revitalizing organizations for a competitive world*, ed R Kilmann and T Covin, Jossey-Bass, San Francisco

Tyson, S (1985) Is this the very model of a modern personnel manager?, *Personnel Management*, May, pp 22–25

Tyson, S (1997) Human resource strategy: a process for managing the contribution of HRM to organizational performance, *International Journal of Human Resource Management*, **8** (3), pp 277–90

Tyson, S and Witcher, M (1994) Human resource strategy emerging from the recession, *Personnel Management*, August, pp 20–23

Ulrich, D (1997) *Human Resource Champions*, Harvard Business School Press, Boston, MA

Ulrich, D (1998) A new mandate for human resources, *Harvard Business Review*, January–February, pp 124–34

Ulrich, D and Brockbank, W (2005) *The HR Value Proposition*, Harvard Press, Cambridge, MA

Ulrich, D and Lake, D (1990) *Organizational Capability: Competing from the inside out*, Wiley, New York

US Department of Labor (1993) *High Performance Work Practices and Work Performance*, US Government Printing Office, Washington, DC

Varma, A, Beatty, R W, Schneier, C E and Ulrich, D O (1999) High performance work systems: exciting discovery or passing fad?, *Human Resource Planning*, **22** (1), pp 26–37

Waddock, S A and Graves, S B (1997) The corporate social performance–financial performance link, *Strategic Management Journal*, **18** (4), pp 303–19

Walker, J W (1992) *Human Resource Strategy*, McGraw-Hill, New York

Walker, P (2007) Develop an effective employer brand, *People Management*, 18 October, pp 44–45

Walton, J (1999) *Strategic Human Resource Development*, Financial Times/Prentice Hall, Harlow

Walton, R E (1985) From control to commitment in the workplace, *Harvard Business Review*, **63**, pp 76–84

Warren, C (2006) Curtain call, *People Management*, 23 March, pp 24–29

Watkin, C (2002) Engage employees to boost performance, *Selection and Development Review*, **18** (2), pp 3–6

Wenger, E and Snyder, W M (2000) Communities of practice: the organizational frontier, *Harvard Business Review*, January–February, pp 33–41

Wernerfelt, B (1984) A resource-based view of the firm, *Strategic Management Journal*, **5** (2), pp 171–80

West, M A, Borrill, C S, Dawson, C, Scully, J, Carter, M, Anelay, S, Patterson, M and Waring, J (2002) The link between the management of employees and patient mortality in acute hospitals, *International Journal of Human Resource Management*, **13** (8), pp 1299–310

Whittington, R (1993) *What Is Strategy and Does It Matter?*, Routledge, London

Wick, C W and Leon, L S (1995) Creating a learning organization: from ideas to action, *Human Resource Management*, Summer, pp 299–311

Wickens, P (1987) *The Road to Nissan*, Macmillan, London

Willmott, H (1993) Strength is ignorance, slavery is freedom: managing culture in modern organizations, *Journal of Management Studies*, **29** (6), pp 515–52

Wood, S (1996) High commitment management and organization in the UK, *International Journal of Human Resource Management*, **7** (1), pp 41–58

Wood, S and Albanese, M (1995) Can we speak of a high commitment management on the shop floor?, *Journal of Management Studies*, **32** (2), pp 215–47

Wood, S, de Menezes, L M and Lasaosa, A (2001) High involvement management and performance, Paper delivered at the Centre for Labour Market Studies, University of Leicester, May

World Business Council for Sustainable Social Development (WBCSSD) (2006) *From Challenge to Opportunity: The role of business in tomorrow's society*, WBCSSD, Geneva

Worley, C, Hitchin, D and Ross, W (1996) *Integrated Strategic Change: How organization development builds competitive advantage*, Addison-Wesley, Reading, MA

Wright, P M and McMahan, G C (1992) Theoretical perspectives for SHRM, *Journal of Management*, **18** (2), pp 295–320

Wright, P M and Snell, S A (1998) Towards a unifying framework for exploring fit and flexibility in strategic human resource management, *Academy of Management Review*, **23** (4), pp 756–72

Wright, P M, Snell, S A and Jacobsen, H H (2004) Current approaches to HR strategies: inside-out versus outside-in, *Human Resource Planning*, **27** (4), pp 36–46

Younger, J, Smallwood, N and Ulrich, D (2007) Developing your organization's brand as a talent developer, *Human Resource Planning*, **30** (2), pp 21–29

Subject index

Author index